GEORGE CLARKE'S
amazing
spaces

Special photography by Ben Anders

GEORGE CLARKE'S
amazing spaces

Quadrille
PUBLISHING

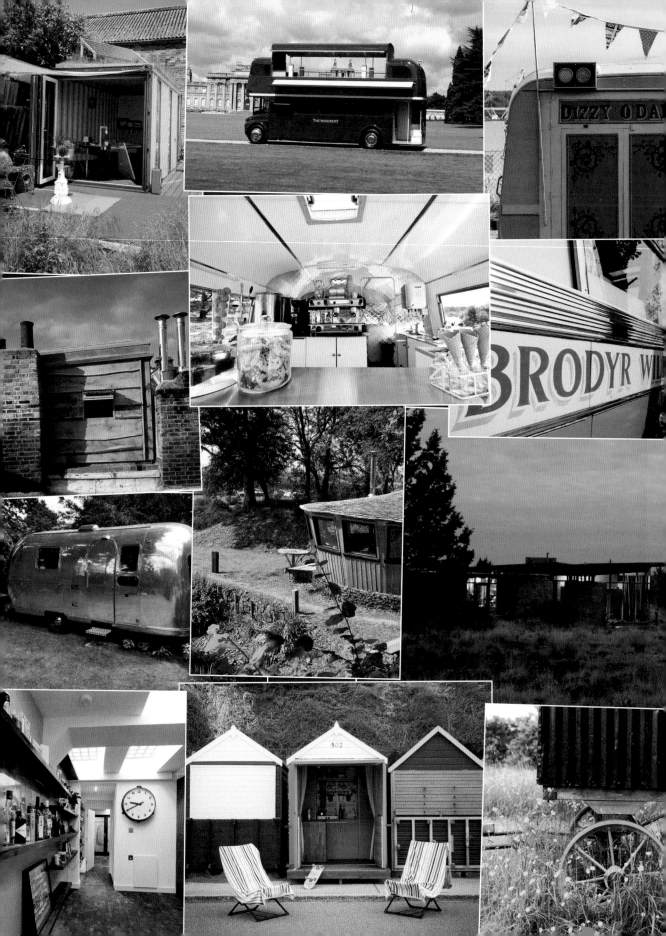

INTRODUCTION

Out there are a great many people who are following their dreams by starting small scale building projects. From secret hideaways at the end of the garden to movable retreats, eco-friendly bolt holes to shipping container homes, these are the people who are squeezing every last inch out of these spaces, making opportunities for themselves and their families to live their lives to the full. They are expressing themselves creatively – starting new businesses and creating workspaces, or making affordable places to live and spaces to have fun with their families and enjoy life.

From the moment the seeds of the idea for 'Amazing Spaces' were sown, I felt excited. It was a great illustration of everything I believe in. How good design, innovation, hard work and energy can fuel honest, human creativity. Here was a chance to connect with elements of architecture, design and building, but with a whole dose of humanity added to it. These are real people, with real projects. Often working with limited funds, but with absolutely no limit to their energy, spirit and determination to create something amazing.

Personally I was so swept up with the idea that I decided to join in; with my own life-changing impulse purchase of a caravan wreck. It was a project that reconnected me with my happy childhood holiday memories, though I needed to convince many people that I hadn't gone mad during the process! The subsequent design and build as well as the search for the right plot of land to put it on were great experiences in their own right. I learnt a lot, and had the opportunity to get to know and work with some great people. I have created some new friendships and at the end of it all I have built my family a unique holiday retreat.

Most importantly, by embarking on my journey to make my perfect caravan space, I got to become part of the group of amazing contributors who are featured within this book. These are all people who have dared to dream big, often without much in the way of practical experience or means. I've noticed that there are key traits shared by them all, creativity and the ability to work on small budgets are common themes (along with the occasional lack of sanity) as well as a general willingness to give things a go, and learn along the way.

Along with the incredible stories of the contributors from the TV series, this book will give you all the inspiration you need to go about making your own amazing space. We have filled it with information to give you plenty of ideas of your own. Whatever project you are thinking of embarking upon – whether creating a new small space of your very own or just going about making a small part of your existing house that bit more special – dare to dream and you too could create yourself a little bit of heaven. Good luck!

George Clarke

For me, co-writing this book has been the result of my very own small space journey. As a working mother and self-employed stylist, figuring out how to manage the long school holidays and juggle the demands of work and childcare was my particular challenge, until the day I spotted a tiny 1970s vintage caravan which looked like a loaf of sliced bread. It was right on the borders of good/bad taste and design and initially I wasn't sure whether I loved it or loathed it. Whatever the case, I knew that I had to have it. Like George's caravan, this purchase turned out to be a life-changer as well as an amazing project in its own right.

That initial seed project of mine gave me a great sense of personal freedom and achievement, along with the chance to discover that these small spaces can offer us so much more than their physical limitations. I love the fact that they give us the opportunity to step outside the routine of our everyday life and start thinking creatively. The enjoyment I have had from meeting the inspiring people who feature on the series and in this book, looking at their awesome projects (whether they cost a good deal or not very much at all) and seeing the way in which they derive so much pleasure from their 'Amazing Spaces' is something that I am delighted to be able to share over the pages that follow.

Jane Field-Lewis

THINKING
UP YOUR OWN
AMAZING SPACE

GETTING STARTED

We all appreciate a bit of space, whether it's physical or giving ourselves the time and stillness to think – to concentrate, have some fun and create a diversion from our everyday routine. For many of us, embracing our own Amazing Space project can provide us with this space, as well as being both an affordable challenge and a great way of engendering a sense of achievement, not to mention a great way of opening up numerous exciting opportunities.

It doesn't matter whether they are high-end or low-end, grand or humble, each space fulfils its specific purpose, providing owners with the qualities they require. And that, really, is the key.

The current trend for small space design is nothing new. For centuries, people from all walks of life have been looking for achievable and interesting solutions to the age-old problem of balancing home, work, leisure time and holidays. Huts and cabins play an important part in the culture of many societies while, if you look back at the past, many owners of stately homes have constructed aesthetically pleasing follies in their gardens as well as small hunting lodges on their estates where shooting parties could be served lunch. The literary greats also knew all about creating amazing spaces: George Bernard Shaw, Virginia Woolf and Roald Dahl all preferred writing in small huts or sheds in their gardens – albeit a short walk but definitely a long journey and a separate place from their main residence.

" The small spaces featured within the following pages are certainly not lacking in ambition or belief. Some even verge on the insane! But they all embody a spirit, which should be encouraged and enjoyed, of limitless possibilities and making the most of life, irrespective of age, income or where you live."

Because these spaces are, more often than not, on a scale that we can all easily relate to, once we've had an idea for one it is relatively easy to set it into action.

The owners of this beach hut (p68) used the money destined to pay for their honeymoon to build this instead – creating a space for the family to enjoy, a place for friends to hang out as well as somewhere to work in the process.

What is new is that we are beginning to think about these little creations as a way of getting away from the mundane, everyday aspects of life. We're starting to think big in these small spaces. To see them as a way of making an active difference to our lives.

Even if the idea of creating your own Amazing Space isn't on your agenda, there is something incredibly liberating about looking at other people's remarkable achievements, especially when they may at first have seemed unrealistic or downright ludicrous. All of the people featured on the series and in this book recognised potential and grasped the opportunity to turn it into reality, often on a relatively modest budget. Reading about their visionary ideas and their subsequent efforts to create them is a thought provoking exercise in itself.

Once that door of possibility has been opened, you can start thinking about the what, how and why. But do try to see the leap of faith that others have taken as an inspiration. Don't put the brakes on your thinking too early on; instead, dream a little and allow the possibilities to happen.

PURPOSE AND *function*

If you are thinking about creating your own Amazing Space opportunity in life, the first question to ask yourself is what is it for? Although most places do have a principal purpose, many are truly multi-functional spaces.

Thinking and planning will take time, but will ensure that the space really does work effectively for multiple uses, rather than not functioning well for any of them. A good starting point is to make a list of what you want the space to provide. Don't worry if it's so long that it seems unreasonable – it's easier to cross items off a list than add things to it, and, with a good deal of thought and careful planning, amazing things can be achieved.

For example, the owners of the Beach Hut (p68), measuring only 0.6m² (6ft²), managed to get it to work successfully as a workspace, a play space with a day bed for their young daughter, a dining room that sits six people, and a relaxing place where friends and family can hang out and enjoy spending time together. That's an impressive achievement, and I'm sure that when they sat down to write their first list of purposes it must have seemed an unobtainable goal.

Both George's Caravan and the Eco Hut (p74 and p156) engage fully with their spectacular natural surroundings.

WHO IS THE SPACE FOR?

This is the next question to ask yourself when you're considering or planning your own Amazing Space. Is it going to be solely for you, or is it a space to share with your family, friends, business or clients? George's caravan adventure, for example, was a particularly family-driven project, as it was based on the values of freedom and simplicity he experienced on his own childhood holidays. They left a legacy that he wanted to pass on to his own children, so that they could share his values through similar experiences.

George's approach to his own Amazing Space journey – creating a caravan holiday home like no other – was for him and his family to all enjoy in equal measure. It's a highly thought out space, both in its design and furnishing, but it never loses sight of the principal objective of being a family-centric space for three generations (plus pets) while still maintaining a top-end credible design aesthetic.

Conversely, if you want a space that is just for you, then creating something highly individual can narrow down your considerations and focus. Tim Sands' woodland cabin is part-shelter, part-workshop, part-retreat, but it's all his own space. However, be warned: there is something about these unique creations that touches people, and you may well find yourself with more friends than you thought you had!

SHOULD THE *project* MAKE SENSE?

I'm almost frightened to write about this, but several of the people whose projects are featured here have dived into these endeavours in a completely impulsive way, without any logical process or step-by-step analysis and decision-making. Sometimes we are suddenly smitten with an idea or inspired by something we see and we act on a whim, on the spur of the moment. Like many before him, George bought his wreck of a static caravan because he felt the enormous pull of nostalgia and was attracted to the design of that particular caravan – it had an appealing shape and, among the rows of nigh-on-identical caravans, it just screamed 'buy me'. The fact that old caravans cost only a few hundred pounds no doubt added to that impulsiveness, but either way this purchase turned out to be a life-changer as well as an amazing project.

Other people are more measured and circumspect in their thinking, taking time to identify the best solution to their needs – whether that's creating an income stream, expanding an existing business or finding an affordable place to live. There is a rational process of thought and discovery here, and, as in the case of the incredible Underground Toilet conversion (p90) into a sleek, modern home, it might even take years of persistence, re-evaluating plans and changing direction to find a way of achieving one's dream when it seems as though there is no way forward at all.

Some people like to feel committed to a project, once they have taken it on, and having unleashed the beast of creativity and obsession they are determined to find a way of carrying it through. The Majestic Bus is a case in point. To most eyes, the bus was past its best, ready only for the scrap yard. Plan A – to turn it into a campervan – had trundled on to the end of the road when the owners realised that it was just too unwieldy a size for British motoring. Plan B was to leave it in situ and turn it into a unique holiday home. To any sane person, that was not only a major leap of faith but there was also the problem of it even being achievable – the bus was a wreck. But for the owners, once that decision had been made there was absolutely no going back. George, too, on discovering that his caravan was damp, made of match wood, blighted with asbestos and with strikingly similar constructional qualities to a sardine can, knew that the idea was bonkers and would inevitably be far more work than he had initially envisaged. But once he'd seen that caravan there was no possibility of changing his mind – he loved the project.

The Exbury Egg (p118) Underground Toilet (p90) and Majestic Bus (p150) are all projects that at times have defied 'common sense', but it is exactly these sorts of spaces that get us thinking about how we can do things differently.

WHERE DO YOU WANT YOUR *space* TO BE?

While many of us start off thinking that we don't have the space for our own Amazing Space project, a hard look should reveal a multitude of potential sites. Projects can be situated in wild open countryside, sprawling rural gardens, urban backyards, or slap bang in the middle of cities – it really is entirely up to you!

If it's important for you to have easy daily access to your project, your back garden or somewhere close by in your neighbourhood might be your best option, not forgetting to look upwards as well as outwards. Likewise, if your project is also your business, it will be important for it be sufficiently nearby in order to deal with its day-to-day running. However, if you plan to use the space just for holidays or weekend breaks, that space can be further away and a reasonable journey is acceptable.

Towns and cities present their own challenges, especially as space is at a premium. There are less opportunities to spread out and lateral space is hard to come by. Later on in this book, you will see two creative solutions to this problem, both of which are spectacular projects. One is a great example of an upward development – a rooftop hut – whereas the other – an underground toilet conversion – is downward under the city streets. Both spaces make you really think outside the box and realise that there are all sorts of possibilities out there if you have an open mind, imagination and the vision and perseverance to make them happen.

Hanging in the 'lost space' between the ground and the treetops, The Treehouse Tent (p134) takes camping to a different level, while The Hut on the Roof (p122) turns the usual urban concept of building a roof extension on its head by building between the chimney tops in a completely different style to the building below.

STARTING FROM SCRATCH OR ADAPTING AN EXISTING SPACE?

Buying an existing structure usually means that you start your project a little further down the line, although the elements you are really buying often amount to no more than a floor, walls and a roof. Whatever form this comes in is up to you. From the experience of the owners featured in this book, very few are ideal. Although they have a notional structure, there are often all sorts of problems and defects, including leaks, poor or no insulation, insufficient light and generally a bad state of repair. All these issues will need addressing. In the case of existing structures, such as shipping containers, caravans and shepherds' huts, they can be relatively inexpensive to buy as well as a great way to get you going. Often they lend the project a style of their own.

Ruth Tidd, for example, found that instant appeal – the initial irresistible, impulsive pull of a project. She spotted a small vintage caravan in a very sorry state of repair, being used as a chicken coop in a farmer's barn. She looked beyond its dilapidated state and, instead, noticed its pretty shape, retro style and potential to become something else, and just asked the owner on the spot if she could have it. Transforming it into the retro coffee and ice cream bar it is today took a huge amount of renovation work, including reinforcing the structure. What she was effectively buying was the style of the caravan. Starting from scratch, it would have been difficult to achieve that authenticity as a replica retro caravan isn't the genuine article.

The other end of the spectrum is the one-off architectural mini-masterpiece, which – if you have this possibility open to you – is a great experience. But don't be fooled into thinking that, just because you are starting from scratch, your project will be without problems. Architecture is an expensive business no matter what the size of your build and, because your space is likely to be a one-off, there will still be a number of unique challenges and decisions to be faced. However, the challenges afford the opportunity for a build that is spectacular both in its vision and execution and because the small size nature of the space allows for a distillation and refinement of design way beyond what you would find in a normal-sized build.

WHAT TYPE OF SPACE SHOULD IT BE?

It's a strange fact, but limiting yourself to a small space not only forces you to think more creatively about the space itself but also about the things that you can put in it. For many of those who undertook the Amazing Spaces projects within this book, the act of spending time in simpler spaces reminded them that we can be happy and fulfilled with fewer things. By reducing the belongings that surrounded them to just the essentials or those that had special significance they were able to create more meaningful environments.

The first thing you should consider when planning your space is how to get your basic needs sorted – comfort and warmth. It's interesting that a number of the Amazing Spaces featured in this book have wood burning stoves. They suit these small spaces, whatever their style and location, and the appeal of tending a fire and sitting beside it, warming your toes, cannot be denied. The other essential things to consider are the quality of the light, how you move around the space, and fitting in the key items you need for the space to function properly.

After these essentials have been considered, you will need to think about the style of your space. Small-build projects can offer you more freedom to experiment and think outside the box, especially if they are not part of or attached to your home. You can design and style them in a totally different way and even indulge your fantasies, whether it's a 'hut on the roof' of your house in the city, a rustic tree house or cabin, or a funkadelic nightclub-styled Airstream at the end of your garden. Feeling liberated to do something really different is both rare and wonderful. It's an opportunity to create a space and style that truly represents you as an individual, rather than having to follow convention. These little spaces have their own confidence and character.

Wood burning stoves come in differing designs and sizes to suit the style of your build. The traditional Shepherd's Hut (p100) has an authentic rounded 'tortoise' stove whereas George's Caravan (p74) features a smaller, rounder modern wood burner.

CREATING YOUR OWN
look AND *style*

Scrapbooks and mood boards can provide a common thread to identifying the sort of look you want to create. They have helped many of the projects in this book find their form and style. It is difficult, even for professionals, to totally visualise how an idea might work in practice, so starting to visually collect a range of ideas can help us all. Online visual blogs and photo-sharing websites provide a more contemporary take on a traditional scrapbook format. Tim Sands, when planning his Eco Hut, used his to collect ideas not only for styling the interior but also for the whole project. Sometimes it only takes one element to get you started; it may be a photograph, an object, a film or even something more intangible, like a feeling. It could even evolve through a natural process of working with the pre-existing colours, textures and materials that are already part of the space.

Even if you think that being creative isn't one of your core skills, there will still be things you instinctively like or don't like, things that make you feel comfortable and others that make you feel awkward. Start to take notice of them. It's also important to enjoy the whole process and take time out to think it through. Considering different style options – discounting some along the way while hanging on to the ones that resonate – can seem like hard work at the time but will eventually end up leaving you in a good place.

The process of refining and distilling all these elements down to a certain style is what all the owners of the projects in this book have done, and the pleasure they have derived from creating these projects goes way beyond their size. Imbued with their individual dreams, endeavours, and small solutions to the big challenges in life, the spaces they have created are filled with spirit, and provide the perfect inspiration for anyone looking to get out and do the same themselves.

A **MOOD BOARD** is a great way of gathering together pictures that resonate with your ideas for a project and inspiring a train of creative thought, but it is slightly unoriginal to copy these pictures wholesale. Instead, use them as a starting point and then look closer. Ask yourself what you really like about them. Is it the colours? The form? The light? The atmosphere? Its practicality?

Stick the picture on your mood board and, using a chunky marker pen, draw an arrow to the elements that are particularly appealing to you. This is often the moment when inspiration starts to take form. Also, look at sources other than the obvious ones — nature, history and art.

INSPIRATION ESSENTIALS

The following are **William Hardie's** *– master craftsman and designer of George's Caravan –* **top tips** *for approaching a new project:*

1 Good ideas tend to be collaborative in nature – a team effort. Inspiration might come from anywhere, when you're least expecting it. For instance, someone might say: 'Hey, I read this interesting feature about a canal boat...', or something might just pop up in the course of a discussion that sows the seed of a brilliant new idea.

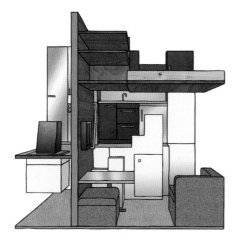

2 When designing something, I find it helpful to push my thoughts to the limit and not to be frightened or discouraged by what seems impossible. By allowing myself a free rein to think an idea through to its extreme, I know what I can reject as well as exploring it to the full in the knowledge that I haven't missed something I should have considered.

3 Before committing anything to a computer drawing, I like to think, draw and sketch. When you change even just one small element of a design, it tends to affect everything else. Although some fortunate people can think through three dimensions in their heads, others can't, and you must find out what works best for you.

4 It is a useful exercise to create a life-size mock-up of the space, using any objects or pieces of furniture to hand, sheets of cardboard or wooden planks – whatever's lying around – to get an accurate idea of how the space might work.

5 I'm a great believer in eureka moments – but they only come through thinking ideas through to their logical conclusions. You have to keep chewing them over, really exploring them from all possible angles. It's almost a scientific process, and you must persevere and keep going to the bitter end. Inspired solutions don't come from sitting around just waiting for an idea to present itself!

6 With any creative work or design project, it's only natural to worry that perhaps a great idea won't come. However, sometimes you find that inspiration has crept up on you but you've just been too preoccupied to notice it. It may just take a passing remark in an everyday conversation for you to realise what you already knew but hadn't yet acknowledged.

7 Don't worry too much about 'thinking outside the box' at first, just start thinking. When you've thought of something, you can always find a box to put it in.

8 There's a danger in looking too much at references and other people's interpretations and work. Truly great ideas come from original sources and you need to consider unlikely sources. Thus if you are thinking about different types of shelters, look at a snail, a termite house or even a wasps' nest rather than just another architect's solution.

9 I'm a great believer in the origins in things, especially history and the natural world. They can provide, often through spurious links, great ideas. Good design has content that makes sense, so do your research thoroughly and look at what history or nature has done to overcome problems.

10 Playfulness and humour are really important elements when creating an original space. Humour doesn't have to be frivolous and can lead to seriously great design – think of that wry smile when someone recognises a clever detail. And, lastly, if you really love what you're doing, it will be evident in the final structure and its styling.

After building my caravan and creating my dream escape I had to consider what my next project should be. I didn't have to think too hard – I've always been completely obsessed with tree houses. They combine fantastical elements, with nature playing a lead role, and bring with them the potential to create something totally individual and unique. They are not just exciting and challenging from a design point of view but are equally testing in terms of their construction and engineering.

Having hit upon the idea I travelled to the amazing Tree House Hotel in Sweden, where I saw some incredible interpretations that really inspired me to get tackling one myself. Looking at the remarkable forms and materials used here was so uplifting and exciting – each of the tree houses has a sense of fun, escape and adventure that is just breathtaking. For me there is nothing like seeing and experiencing something to get a real sense of inspiration, so whatever your build happens to be, try to search out those sources of great design to get your creative juices flowing and the ideas forming. Before you know it you'll be creating something equally spectacular too.

MOVABLE SPACES

What is it about vehicles? Is it that they seem to bring with them the essence of joy and the possibility of freedom and change? The sense that life doesn't always need to be static, whether literally or metaphorically. In this chapter you'll find a wide variety of different projects that embrace this sense of freedom – caravans become backyard nightclubs, chic coffee/ice cream bar businesses or even holiday homes for those fancying a bit of the travelling lifestyle without the life on the road.

THE *ice cream* CARAVAN

ALTHOUGH THIS CARAVAN HAS NO DOUBT BEEN ON SOME SPECTACULAR JOURNEYS IN THE PAST, THIS LATEST ONE VERGES ON THE JAW-DROPPING AND SHOWS THAT SMALL SPACES DON'T HAVE TO MEAN SECOND HOMES – THEY CAN BE SET OUT TO WORK TOO.

A tiny 1.8 x 2.7m (6 x 9ft), this 1957 Bluebird Eurocamper has had an eventful life. Having started out as a happy little holiday home, several decades later it had begun to look rather sad, full of mould, straw and wasps' nests, and seemingly destined to eke out the rest of its days as a humble chicken coop on a farmyard.

Its saviour came in the form of Ruth Tidd – a woman of undoubted vision and determination – who spotted its inherent beauty, recognised its potential and persuaded the farmer who owned it to part with it – if she bought him a replacement chicken coop in return. (Sometimes you just have to ask.) Now this was a project that was really crying out for imagination, and Ruth had a plan – to transform the caravan into her new business venture. An ardent movie fan who revelled in the glamour of the 1950s, she decided to restore and re-invent it as a stylish travelling ice cream soda bar and coffee shop.

BEFORE...

"This project was like a rollercoaster ride but it was such a good one to get on ... and at the end there's candy floss!"

RUTH TIDD – OWNER

The Plan

When it came to turning the caravan into a working mobile food business, Ruth already knew what she was doing – having previously run a successful event catering business out of a vintage Carlight caravan. Ruth understood her market and foresaw that the trends for vintage style and street food were still growing in popularity. Her plan for the new caravan was to fit it out and use it to sell authentic Italian coffee, ice cream floats, traditional teas and home-made cakes. It was to be a hybrid of 1950s glamour, quality food, coffee, ice cream and fun.

Ruth decided to commission the garage that had restored her Carlight to renovate and customise the new caravan. Patronised by classic car aficionados, she not only had confidence in the quality of their workmanship but she also knew that she could work with them, even if they did occasionally raise their eyebrows at some of her more quirky requests.

Structure

This tiny, lightweight caravan was built during a new era of mass production and innovation to make caravans more accessible to the growing consumer market. Changes in manufacturing techniques coincided with new labour laws, and to many families of the time these caravans embodied a sense of freedom as well as a means of taking affordable annual holidays. There was something optimistic about their design, large windows and light interiors, and they could also be towed easily behind a standard family saloon car.

Design-wise, this little caravan reflects the distinctive style of the 1950s and 1960s. Possessing less decorative features than its predecessors, it is simple and modern with straighter vertical lines that gently converge towards the roof line, creating a simple clean shape that is more accommodating to fit out.

Design and style

With a keen visual sense and an appreciation of the usefulness of collecting ideas via mood boards, Ruth likes to gather images of things that inspire her, sometimes with no end use in mind. From books and magazines to the internet and newspapers, she files pictures and articles. She even describes her fridge door as her own Pinterest board!

Ruth found herself drawn to certain images and loved the sexiness of the Italian coffee bars of the 1950s with their cool-looking people perched on bar stools, as well as the American ice cream parlours of the same period. It was the hybrid of these two phenomena that emerged as the design brief for both the interior and exterior of the caravan as well as the nature of the business. This project was going to be all about fun, glamour and optimism.

AMAZING SPACE ESSENTIALS

1 If you are considering repurposing an existing vehicle then do ensure that it is structurally sound – major structural work costs money!

2 Do your due diligence and research potential suppliers really thoroughly to ensure you get the best price and quality.

3 If someone else is doing the conversion work for you, then make sure that you project-manage it to the best of your ability.

4 Ensure all the materials you choose are durable and long lasting. Don't skimp on them.

Traditional perspex cake stands, soda glasses, a gumball machine and a state-of-the-art coffee machine were purchased either online or at vintage fairs.

Ruth's first caravan had been painted a duck egg blue, so this new addition to the family needed a harmonious and complementary colour. Pastel pink, much loved in the post-war 1950s and used in ceramics, interiors and fashion, seemed a great idea, and Ruth tracked down a retro car paint supplier. It looks brilliant with the steel and had her desired 1950s feeling.

Materials and techniques

Although the aesthetics of this caravan were exactly what Ruth was looking for, a great deal needed to be done to bring it up to the standards necessary for a catering business. Structurally, the floor, walls and ceiling all needed to be reinforced to make it strong enough for purpose. In addition, the entire caravan had to be properly sealed to keep out the damp, and the window glass replaced with safety glass. And if that wasn't enough, the gas supply had to meet the required standards for installation, as did the electrics.

Stainless steel is a major feature of the interior and exterior. Ruth chose it for its aesthetic, practical and food hygiene properties as well as the distinctive colour palette inspired by American cars of the period – pastels, cream and, of course, chrome bumpers and hubcaps. The weight of the caravan meant that the tyres and towing gear had to be up to scratch, too, and the quilted steel cladding Ruth had chosen for the exterior needed to be a precise fit and shape. Ruth took the templates to the fabricators to be cut to size. There was no room for error as everything had to be millimetre perfect.

With the project taking four months and going twice over budget, Ruth's approach was to think of it as a building and project manage the process in the same way. This was a custom build as Ruth values a quality finish, and high standards of workmanship and superior materials were essential if the caravan and the business were both to flourish and endure.

Now finished, The Ice Cream Caravan is out to work. Popular at weddings and local events, it is also in demand for magazine and advertising photo-shoots. Its cute retro styling and ability to create an atmosphere add to its attraction.

Rather than create a small serving area, Ruth was keen to engage her customers, both in terms of serving them quickly and also that they could share in the 'caravan' experience.

COMPACT
KITCHENS

1 This tiny kitchen would look even smaller if it was boxed in. Storing goods neatly and in plain sight like this helps to engages the eye, while also making things easy to find.

2 In this kitchen full use is made of the available vertical space. Hanging rails are used at differing heights for storage of pots and pans, while feature lighting and the tiling, which runs all the way up the walls, draws the eye upwards.

3 A super compact kitchen like this presents challenges to fit in the basics. Notice here the small wall-hung, fold down table, which doubles as a food prep area.

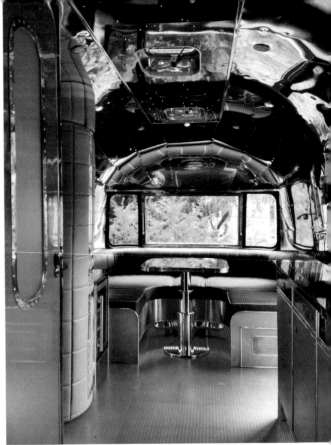

THE AIRSTREAM

Airstreams are the rock 'n' roll of the caravan world. A classic piece of American design, they cannot help but catch the eye and create interest wherever they go. Yet parked at the end of a very short walk in its owners' back garden, this 1971 'land yacht' Airstream's travelling days are over. Refitted and restored, it has been transformed into a unique nightclub and party piece, so no late-night cabs are needed to get home after a big night out.

Most small-space designs provide an opportunity to express your own personal taste and style, taking on whatever form you wish, from the rustic and simple to the high-end and super glossy. This Airstream is a fabulous example of the latter. It's a fun palace – highly finished and well thought out – and by using sleek materials and dazzling finishes, it's super shiny in all respects.

IN THE WORLD OF SMALL DESIGN, THE AIRSTREAM CARAVAN IS AS ICONIC AS THE VW CAMPERVAN. HERE, THIS PIECE OF GLORIOUS AMERICANA HAS BEEN TRANSFORMED INTO SOMETHING TRULY AMAZING – A NIGHTCLUB AT THE END OF THE GARDEN.

The Plan

Exuding self-confidence and glamour, the Airstream trailer is a design icon, as American as apple pie. Its metal exterior and distinctive shape with curved ends, windows and doors are the stuff of dreams for many who might not usually give a caravan a second look. Because of this inherent beauty, Airstream exteriors tend to be restored in a sympathetic manner and are rarely changed or adapted. Owners seem to be happier tinkering with and redesigning the interior space, sometimes restoring it in an authentic way but also letting rip, so it takes on a whole new look.

In this case the owner Bernard, falls very much into the latter camp, his soul aim was to create a nightclub in his garden, complete with a funky interior. His inspiration point, which effectively became his brief to the designer, was a lava lamp. For Bernard this represented aspects of the feel and look he had in mind: shiny metal, high-spec finish with a psychedelic, fun and slightly louche feel. Even the 1960s colour palette of the liquid in the lamp itself – lavender, plum and orange – proved inspirational, leading to a private party space stylised with 1960s and 1970s influences, colours and textures, along with hints of psychedelia and touches of punk rock. There wasn't going to be any subtlety here!

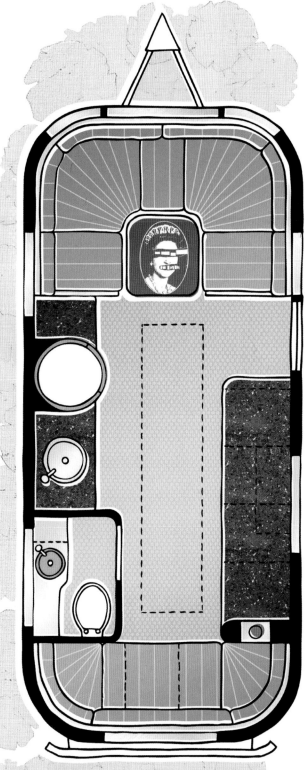

The highly reflective quality of The Airstream's exterior shouts 'look at me', but it also has an ability to blend in to its environment as the exterior reflects its surroundings. Here, at the end of this domestic garden, The Airstream's highly polished and riveted exterior reflects the leaves, sky and nature at its best.

Interior

From this initial lava lamp brief, Kathy Morrison, designer on the project and co-owner of the Airstream restoration company, began to collate a moodboard. This included samples of the materials to be used in the interior, from lavender leather to orange laminate.

The trailer is, in effect, an open-plan space, with a small kitchen area and enclosed bathroom located along its long side. The main seating area, a curved bench seat upholstered in lavender leather, is at one end. The 'God Save the Queen' graphic punk rock stencil designed table within the curve rises and falls hydraulically to become the base for a bed, with additional cushions to complete the mattress.

A central feature of the design is a curved, built-in cocktail cabinet, using highly finished and reflective materials. The reflections of the multicoloured glasses and spirits dance inside the lit-up cabinet.

The complete internal and external restoration of this 1971 'land yacht' Airstream took nine months and a great deal of money, ambition and determination, including the cost of a crane to lift it over the house into the back garden. This space was designed purely for fun and pleasure – a place where Bernard, the owner, could entertain his business clients and guests. He wanted it to look and feel as funky as possible but there are elements of nostalgia, too, mixed up and stylised with super gloss and fantasy. As Bernard rightly describes it: 'It's a fun palace in here'.

The curve of The Airstream's windows, door and wheel arches, along with the curved interior walls, dictate what can be done inside. In this case, the budget was considerable but a successful restoration can be achieved with a more modest sum of money – although you may have to forgo some details and mod-cons, such as air conditioning and under-floor heating.

Highly reflective surfaces, and multi-directional lighting from different sources combine to create this full-on party space interior. With a hi-gloss look like this it is essential that the finishes are of a very high standard, as anything less than perfect will be obvious to the eye.

AMAZING SPACE ESSENTIALS

This is an entrancing glimpse into the world of fully restored Airstreams. However, taking on a challenge like this is not for the faint-hearted, unskilled or shallow of pocket. From the point of view of the restorer, there are several important considerations before embarking on a project of this kind.

1 Bear in mind the practicalities of restoring or redesigning a vehicle like this. If you are strapped for cash, for example, you can keep the original interior and renovate it rather than embarking on a major redesign as per this impressive project.

2 Check your intended purchase carefully before committing to buying. It's essential your vehicle has a good clean exterior and a solid underbelly. Many will have some evidence of rot on the floor near the

bathroom and kitchen, so it's best to check carefully and seek advice from an expert before you buy.

3 Be aware that a full Airstream renovation is not for amateurs; you need a variety of skills, including metal work, carpentry, electrics and plumbing.

4 Safety first: get a gas safety check done immediately by a certified professional and, similarly, check the electrics.

5 If you are hoping to tow your vehicle, check that you have the appropriate legislation regarding the size of trailer, the towing vehicle necessary and the type of licence required, along with any mechanical aspects, such as the electrics, towing mechanism and brakes.

1 Despite their distinctive exteriors, Airstreams interiors take very well to being reimagined in many different ways and styles. Using classic materials and styling, gingham fabrics, shiny chrome, leatherette and a black and white checkerboard floor, this Airstream pulls together elements of both wholesome 1950s Americana and classic diner style.

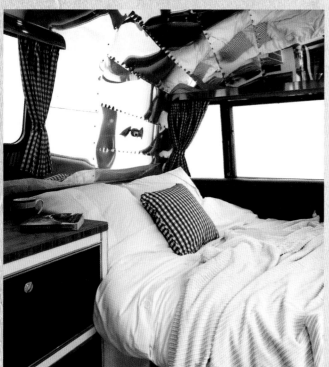

2 This Airstream achieves a completely different look and feel. Note how, by using simpler finishes and by covering the highly reflective interior chrome roof, a simpler, cleaner and more architectural look has been created.

Curved edges are used throughout the design, which open the space up and allow it to flow, while the polished wood (which bounces light around the Airstream), simple cabinetry and bright, breezy colour palette impart a mid-century Scandivian aesthetic to the interior.

THE ROSEBERY

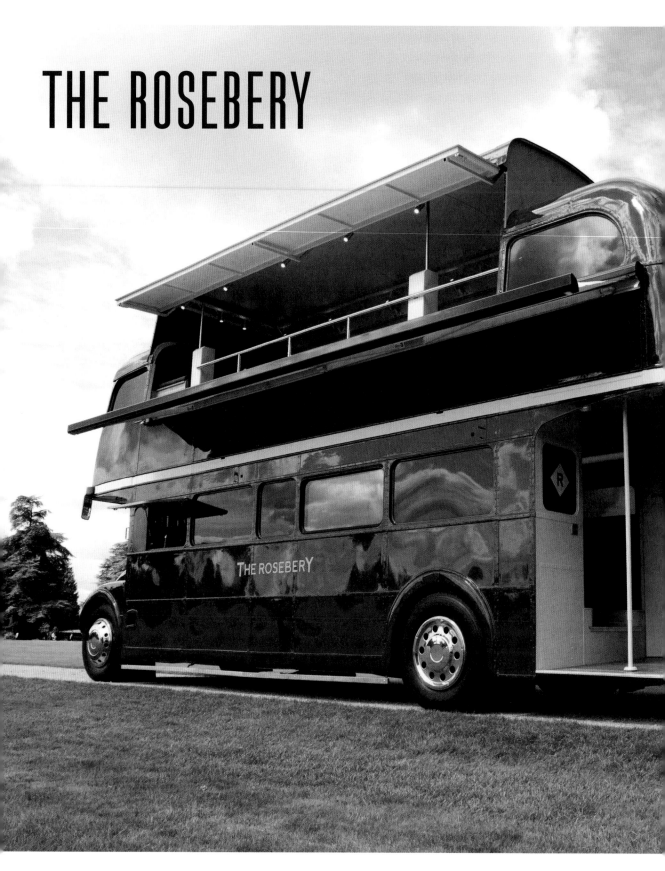

Developed between 1947 and 1955, the Routemaster bus was visionary for the time. Tasked to be a durable and efficient means of public transport around the busy congested streets of London, its highly functional design and open-platform were loved by its travelling customers right up until its eventual retirement in 2005.

This imaginative and exceptionally stylish conversion has done its best to retain the distinctive qualities of the iconic original bus. Using skilled craftsmen accustomed to working on the upholstery of luxury British cars, the slick interior finish of this restaurant and cocktail bar is breathtaking, while the major structural transformation has been the installation of hydraulic jacks that allow the roof to lift and become a canopy – converting the upstairs into a light and airy, but still spectacularly glamorous, space.

FISHERTON FARM

For centuries, extraordinary gypsy horse-drawn caravans have provided transport and (more importantly) cosy homes for whole families. Gavin and Jemma Dicken caught the bug for these charming caravans, known as vardoes, when they spotted an advert for one in their local paper. The owners of a farm with rare-breed cattle and sheep, they thought a gypsy caravan would make an amazing playhouse for their two children as well as doubling up as a spare bedroom for house guests.

As their unique 'spare room' became more and more popular with children and guests alike, Gavin and Jemma spotted the potential of building a business to enable more people to share this unique experience. Sourcing the caravans took some time: the Romany community are rightly, protective of their heritage and buying a vardo is not straightforward. Through a trusted local intermediary, they purchased the three vardoes they own today – Big Ted, Red Rum and Little Gem.

WHEN TRYING TO CREATE SOMETHING NEW, IT'S OFTEN ADVISABLE TO LOOK BACK IN TIME TO SEE IF HISTORY CAN OFFER ANY INSPIRATION.

The Plan

Gavin and Jemma's aim was to create an authentic rural experience for their guests. Their farm provided an ideal location in glorious rolling countryside, and using the caravans as accommodation for holiday rentals would enable them to diversify their business, providing them with an additional income stream. Gradually, a plan evolved to create a private camping area around the three caravans, with its own outdoor kitchen, showers and living area.

Later appropriated by the Romany gypsy community, Vardoes were used originally in France by travelling circus showmen. These men often custom-built their own wagons, embellishing them elaborately to give them their own distinctive identity.

RED RUM

AMAZING SPACE ESSENTIALS

1 Whatever your project, don't dive in straight away. Take your time. An old, reclaimed vehicle in particular has its own personality, so sit in it, absorb it, celebrate in it, and then get dreaming...

2 Bring out all the bits and pieces you have squirreled away from your travels – this is the perfect opportunity to use them.

3 Try to use fabrics in a different way... whether that's using towels for curtains or restitching cushion covers. Reinvent things.

4 Make sure that your environment reflects where you are and who you are. For example, the three caravans here proudly display the sheepskins that Gavin and Jemma produce themselves.

5 If your project has bed space, make sure the beds are big, strong and luxuriously snuggly.

6 Maximise your space by removing cupboards where you have them and replacing them with shelves instead.

7 Scout around charity shops for all the little fittings, such as hooks, mirrors and vases, you'll need to make your space functional.

8 If you have purchased a Romany caravan, sand and stain to enhance the woods within the wagons, gloss floors and benches to reflect light.

9 Keep outdoors, outdoors – leaving boots, coats and smelly socks outside will make a big difference to the quality of your inside space.

10 If your project is in the big outdoors, don't forget to invest in solar desk lamps. They makes great mood lighting for about 4 hours (so long as you remember to charge them!).

BIG TED

Right from the start, Gavin and Jemma decided that they wanted to keep both the interior and exteriors of their vardoes as original as possible. They are unique vehicles and their original purpose – as the ultimate small space for living and travelling – was just what Gavin and Jemma were seeking. Thorough research was essential in order to conserve and repair the caravans in the most appropriate way.

However, while staying faithful to their original purpose and appearance, Gavin and Jemma wanted to provide their guests with the modern comforts and a touch of luxury that they would expect. The result is not a strict recreation of the authentic Romany lifestyle but a contemporary taster in the style of a glamping holiday.

Exteriors

The caravan exteriors were a real labour of love, needing rubbing down and repairing before painstaking repainting. Only 'Little Gem' retains its original brilliant primary green exterior paintwork, which Jemma found so exhilarating that she decided to run it through to the interior with a basic bold colour scheme.

LITTLE GEM

Interiors

The wagon interiors are the ultimate manifestation of a compact travelling and living space – with every possible nook and cranny utilised to the full.

Each caravan is equipped with a high double bed with room below for extra sleeping space or storage. The beds either pull out over a slatted wooden base, or fold out to become a regular double size.

To make the most of the available space, not only is the seating built in, with bench-style seats fixed to the side walls, but all the cupboards and beds are built-in fixtures too.

Wood burning stoves provide the caravan's warmth in winter, while the windows and doors can be opened at either end of each caravan to allow the breeze through on a hot summer's day.

Styling and decoration

An accomplished artist, Jemma has travelled extensively, soaking up inspiration along the way. Her plan was to paint and style each of the wagons to create its own individual character, adding a sense of luxury wherever possible.

The two key crafts of the caravan builds were carpentry and decorative artwork, and although Jemma was keen to respect the traditional Romany folk art tradition, decorative styles and techniques, she also wanted some freedom of expression in tackling the exterior paintwork and interior styling. Her objective was to create a look that was as eye-catching and beautiful as possible while retaining the intrinsic charm and atmosphere of the vardoes. For her, each caravan had its own personality, no matter what condition it arrived in, and she wanted to enhance this rather than change it.

The interior of 'Red Rum' reflects traditional styles, with small-pattern repeat fabrics, including gingham and patchwork.

Jemma and Gavin removed the usual cupboards that sit under the main bed, thereby maximising space to create new room to store slide-out children's beds.

USING
PATTERN

1 Mixing pattern can quickly create a confident but relaxed atmosphere. The key item in this bedroom image is the blanket. Its orange tones and geometric pattern are echoed in the florals and loose stripes on the cushions, while the loose white embroidered sheet and the additional white pillow give the patterns room to breathe.

2 It can be refreshing to see pattern where you would least expect it. The patterned wallpaper in this kitchen has been applied as if the units were a flat wall.

3 When working to find pattern combinations that sit well together, matching colours might seem like the approach. Not so. In this room the curve of the stylised leaf shape in the wallpaper is echoed in the delicate branch of the cushion, which works despite the difference in colour.

THE
Wessex Rose

THERE ARE TIMES IN LIFE THAT JUST FEEL RIPE FOR CHANGE, BUT PUTTING OUR IMPULSES INTO PRACTICE IS NEVER EASY. THE COUPLE BEHIND THIS BUILD HAVE DONE SO ON A MASSIVE SCALE – BEGINNING A NEW LIFE AND BUSINESS AS WELL AS EMBARKING ON A MAJOR RENOVATION PROJECT.

David and his wife Karen wanted – and needed – a complete lifestyle change. They both had stressful and intense jobs, working long hours, and had gradually come to the realisation that this was not what life should be about. When Karen received notice that she was going to be made redundant, the timing seemed right to hatch a new 10-year plan.

They wanted to work together, doing something totally different from their past employment. Having both always enjoyed the great outdoors they initially thought of running a caravan site, but the capital investment for this was too big. It was seeing a short television feature about a hotel boat that sparked their brilliant new idea. The concept resonated with them, and they started to formulate a detailed business plan for a narrow boat hotel to see if it would be financially viable.

Because of the low height of many of the tunnels and bridges along the canal, the roof deck needs to be collapsible as the head clearance is limited. The balustrades of the terrace have been designed to fold completely flat as do the directors chairs on the deck.

The Plan

As part of their business plan, David and Karen researched the market thoroughly – in the process discovering that there was only one other broad-beam hotel operating in the north of Britain. While investigating the canal network, they came across the Kennet and Avon canal, linking Bristol to London. This canal was built using the shortest possible route across southern England. As a result, it runs through some of the most stunning scenery and was the perfect location for their budding business.

David and Karen don't waste time procrastinating – they get on and do things. Consequently, they both learnt to be qualified helmsmen, and, after securing the necessary finance, started working on transforming their dream into a reality. As it was not possible to buy the sort of boat they wanted, having one built specially to order was the only way to proceed. They located and briefed the builder of the other hotel boat operating in the north, but this commission was different and much bigger. At 21m (70ft) long and 3.8m (12ft 6in) wide, weighing in at 50 tons, The Wessex Rose was to be the largest canal boat in England.

Throughout the design utilises clever solutions to maximise the available space – every nook and cranny has been used as additional storage.

Design and materials

The process of designing and building the boat took place in two distinct stages. To begin, a hull builder constructed the hull out of 22 tons of steel. After the hull construction, the boat builder fitted out and configured the internal space as well as working out and overseeing the engineering and technological elements of the project. The materials used were British sourced wherever possible, and included a great deal of environmentally friendly seasoned oak, which the boat builders machined in their own workshops.

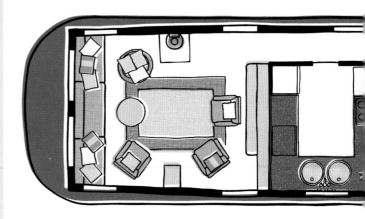

AMAZING SPACE ESSENTIALS

1 Plan in advance and in minute detail. And don't be worried that, even when you do, you'll be surprised at how much you have missed!

2 Allow yourself time. Projects always take a lot longer than you anticipate.

3 Be sure to draw up an accurate and detailed budget and always add a contingency fund for unforeseen expenses. No matter how good your forecasting, you will use the contingency.

4 Build good working relationships with suppliers and rely on their expertise and advice – be prepared to compromise and bend a little as maintaining the relationship will pay dividends in the long term.

5 Expect knocks and setbacks – don't be disheartened but accept them as nothing more than challenges, and don't give up at the first hurdle. It's your unfailing self-belief that will make your dream a reality.

The furniture and cabinetry was all custom-built for this project.

No project worth doing is ever going to be quick and easy, and this was no exception. The path from starting to get serious about the idea to the actual launch day took 14 months. Whatever the level of detailed planning and discussion that goes into such complex projects, it is always beneficial if someone is on hand to make design decisions as problems and needs arise. Therefore the couple moved to be nearer to the boat build rather than managing the process from a distance.

Interior and styling

The Wessex Rose can accommodate a maximum of six guests in three bedrooms as well as providing a lounge and roof deck area. Storage space is always at a premium on a boat, and so the bedrooms have been designed with as much built-in storage as possible. Each has a small wardrobe and chest of drawers that finishes at waist height to provide a surface area too. The bedrooms are each panelled in oak, and each has an ensuite bathroom, with a bespoke etched glass door. All the fabric tones in the bedrooms are cool neutrals and the oak itself is light toned, the overall feel is calm and comfortable, and the high level of finish to the joinery and to the soft furnishings subtly help create a relaxing space.

The lounge is at the front of the boat, and has a small steel stove as a focal point. A section of the roof is a retractable sunroof, operated by a button and the windows and two hatches can all be fully opened to transform this into an indoor/outdoor space. The oak floor, and blues, stone and cream colour scheme are subtle, in truth this needs to be a comfortable relaxing

space but still outward looking, to the water, wildlife and location itself.

For David and Karen, the project has been a complete lifestyle change. Having downsized from a four-bedroom house, their own personal space on the boat is now 3 x 3m (10 x 10ft). Naturally, this life-changing transition resulted in some serious and comprehensive decluttering. But sometimes living small and lean and designing our lives in a healthier and happier way can be more fulfilling – there are so many things we really can do without. As the couple maintain: 'It makes you realise that life, memories and values are more important than material things'. Now they are more in control of their destiny with a different view of life: a fresh start, a new business and the chance to work for themselves.

Although many new narrow boats are still built, very few 'wide beam' boats like The Wessex Rose are constructed. These boats are just that: about 1–2m (3–6ft) wider than a conventional narrow boat, providing the much needed internal living space for David and Karen's floating hotel.

One of the major design challenges for The Wessex Rose was how to create a good-sized living area that connected with the outside. The solution – a lounge fitted with a large sunroof which opens up completely – gives the feeling of space and openness that was needed, enabling guests to enjoy the view and weather as they travel.

THE LAND ROVER
COCKTAIL BAR

IT IS CLEAR THAT YOU NEED TO HAVE SOME SERIOUS IMAGINATION TO ENVISAGE A BEATEN UP, WORN OUT LAND ROVER AS A COCKTAIL BAR. YOU ALSO NEED A WILLINGNESS TO TACKLE MAJOR PRACTICAL CHALLENGES TO MAKE THAT DREAM A REALITY. THIS IS ONE OF THOSE PROJECTS THAT DEMANDS AN ENORMOUS AMOUNT OF VISION AND CHARACTER.

BEFORE...

This Land Rover Defender has undergone a radical transformation. From a rugged and life-worn utility vehicle, more used to a tough existence on rough terrain, it has been converted into a high-end, glossy, mobile cocktail bar. Rew, the instigator of this unique project, is a renowned cocktail maker. His events company plans, arranges and hosts cocktail and bar services in people's homes, at parties and festivals. He was looking for a way to expand and do something completely different – to give his business an edge – and an idiosyncratic, eye-catching, mobile and fun setup seemed a good solution. He considered a range of options, including campervan conversions and even a Routemaster bus, but he wanted something more unusual and eventually fell for the particular charms of the rusty, beaten-up beast that was this 2004 Land Rover Defender.

The Plan

The idea for The Land Rover Cocktail Bar emerged over the course of a dinner conversation, and once the concept had been established, the next decision was to identify which model would be the most appropriate. Rew did his research thoroughly, looking at all the different Land Rover models and their differing specifications and sizes. As he needed space at the back to build the bar section, he chose a Land Rover 130 (the 130 refers to the length of the wheelbase). As the model with the largest platform at the back, this particular vehicle is ideal for adaption to other uses and is often used for conversions. It has a 'crew cab' too – a two-row seating cab at the front – and a pick-up style back-end. As such, Rew felt that it offered the best configuration for his intended purpose.

Searching the country, Rew eventually found an old vehicle that once belonged to the Water Board. It had a canopy on the back and had been bashed about and was horrendously dented, but the Land Rover's renowned strong chassis and relatively simple but sturdy body construction make

it reasonably straightforward to repair and replace body parts. Rew's father was happy to help with the repair work, calling in expert help where necessary. A hard top 'camel back' was fitted, replacing the original canvas, plus new bumpers, and the electrics were checked professionally and signed off. All the bodywork was repaired and even the nuts and bolts were replaced.

The plan was to run the cocktail business out of the back of the vehicle, leaving the cab intact. The design concept was based on that of a Transformer toy (an object that starts with a series of moves before being transformed into something else). The Land Rover would be a conventional road-worthy and regular-looking vehicle but with a back section that would pull out to reveal the bar section that would then be constructed along the long side of the vehicle. The side panels of the camel back would open up to reveal the shelves of glassware and cocktail ingredients and act as a backdrop to a good sized bar area, where people could chill out and enjoy a drink or two.

Design and materials

Rew thought long and hard about what makes a good bar, ergonomically and aesthetically, drawing on his considerable experience of the subject. Applying these principles, he worked through various design possibilities to discover how to use this small unorthodox space to its maximum potential. The idea was to work with the form and design of the original vehicle. Key materials and features would be referenced and the qualities of the Land Rover – sturdiness, use of durable materials and visible fixings – would be adhered to in the design of the bar itself.

The choice of materials, styling and finishing touches all needed considerable thought. Rew didn't want this to be an overly flashy vehicle. Instead, he wanted it to be clean-looking and beefy, masculine and tough – a challenging task, given that this was going to be all about cocktails. With this in mind, he chose a characteristic cross-tread metal for the bar counter surface, a material normally used on the footplates, while the headlights, grilles and rivets are carried through into the design of the bar. A snorkel, which is usually fitted so the vehicle can be driven through water and to direct exhaust gases upwards to prevent the engine flooding, has instead been used as a rubbish chute and drain.

A key consideration with the design of the bar was its need to be easily disassembled and packed away, but also to be sturdy and permanent feeling when in action. A precisely measured, steel framework was fabricated to order and professional standard catering sinks and shelving slots in and links the vertical supports together. The chunky bar surface is sectional and when placed on top is firmly clamped into place.

Projects such as this one require two key attributes – passion and energy – all the while keeping the end destination clearly in mind. Rew admits that a conventional office life was not for him. He is a confident and social person whose philosophy is that if you do what you love in life everything else will fall into place. He has learnt along the way not to let his ideas run away from him, but to deal with the practical challenges and decisions in a step-by-step manner, getting this vehicle functioning purposefully to achieve his goals. Combining tough macho aesthetics with glamorous individually created cocktails, this is one bespoke vehicle that won't need pulling out of that muddy festival field.

The cocktail bar makes great use of the Land Rover's usual fixtures and fittings. The snorkel that usually acts as the vehicle's upright exhaust has been converted into a rubbish chute and drain for excess ice, while the jerry cans that would usually store extra petrol have been converted into speakers for the bar's sound system.

BAR
AREAS

1 Almost any piece of furniture that includes a flat surface can be used to create a home bar area. This one is super simple – a practical and easily achievable way of dressing the space for this specific purpose.

2 We've all spotted that vintage cocktail bar in a second-hand shop looking past its best, but this one has gained pride of place in this modern lounge – its characteristic curved shape, glasses on show and high bar stool creating its own area and atmosphere.

3 Many home 'bar areas' are on show, the bottles and glasses arranged neatly. Here a decorative mirror fronted low cupboard unit has been used for that purpose. It has a glamour of its own and keeps all the essentials together, but has the added advantage of being able to be closed away when you need the space to have a more formal feel.

MULTI-FUNCTIONAL SPACES

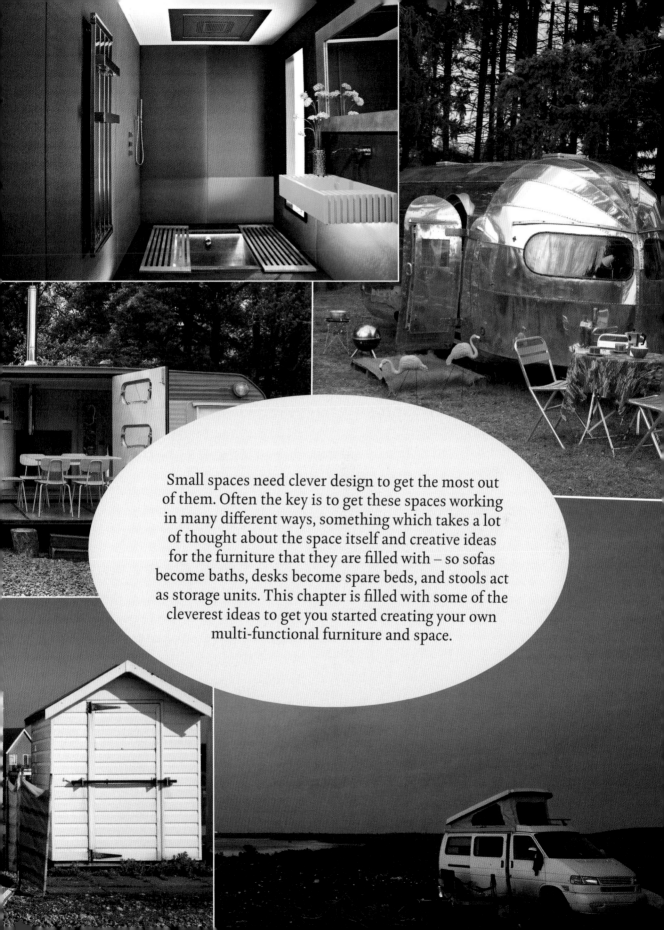

Small spaces need clever design to get the most out of them. Often the key is to get these spaces working in many different ways, something which takes a lot of thought about the space itself and creative ideas for the furniture that they are filled with – so sofas become baths, desks become spare beds, and stools act as storage units. This chapter is filled with some of the cleverest ideas to get you started creating your own multi-functional furniture and space.

THE **LEGO** APARTMENT

You have to be a certain type of person to live happily in a small space such as this, which, of necessity, demands clean lines and a tidy nature! Luckily Christian Shallet is such a man and it was his chance sighting of a flyer advertising an 'attic for sale' that led to this exciting project. Christian fell in love with the space (despite the only access being up a narrow flight of 100 steps), seeing the potential to transform this tiny 24m² (258ft²) 'pigeon hole' into a highly desirable, super-compact apartment.

With its large glass doors opening out to the Barcelona rooftops beyond, this unique one-room studio flat holds plenty of surprises – with the exception of the small table and chairs that sit out on the terrace, every piece of furniture has been built-in specially. Through a combination of clever design and immaculate attention to detail and finishes, Christian has transformed his apartment into one of the most multi-functional spaces in Europe.

BARCELONA IS ONE OF THE MOST BEAUTIFUL CITIES IN THE WORLD. IT'S ALSO HOME TO ONE OF THE MOST EXTRAORDINARILY DESIGNED STUDIO APARTMENTS EVER – PROBABLY THE BEST SPACE I HAVE EVER SEEN IN TERMS OF MAKING EVERY SQUARE CENTIMETRE WORK.

The Plan

Christian runs several creative businesses and although he admits to not being a particularly homely sort of person, dreamt of having his own affordable, practical living space. He travels extensively for work and therefore the apartment had to be functional, basic and not excessive in any way.

The inspiration for the project came from two main sources. Christian grew up on the shores of Lake Constance in Austria and loved the layout of boat interiors, while another important influence was the design of Japanese houses, where space is at a premium. Along with this, Christian introduced ideas from the work of architectural greats, such as Mies Van de Rohe, Le Corbusier and the Bauhaus movement that focused on making the most of tiny living spaces.

Christian's starting point was to list all the items he wanted to include in his home in the most minute detail – even T-shirts, shorts, socks, underwear, DVDs and sports equipment. He then measured the minimum space that each group required and began to allocate cupboards and storage space accordingly.

Lots of brainstorming and many sketches later, Christian's ideas started to take form as he attempted to squeeze a house into a space approximately the same size as most people's hallways. He knew that there was not enough space for the usual items – even a bed and a table – so logic dictated that they couldn't be permanent fixtures and would have to be stowed away. It was also clear that he would need adequate storage for bedding and such like, so every small space – even the step up to the terrace – would have to be utilised.

Although Christian had the vision, he knew his limitations. He needed professional advice to execute his plan, so he enlisted architect Barbara Appolloni to convert his ideas and thoughts into the technical drawings that would turn his dream into a practical reality. From this sound base, he was able to brief skilled teams to carry out the works.

BEFORE...

"For me, the key approach was to ask one very simple question: what are the essentials of everyday living? The answers I came up with were somewhere to cook, wash, sit and sleep."

CHRISTIAN SHALLET – OWNER

In this apartment every possible scrap of space, both inside and out, is made to work as hard as possible. And yet, rather than seeming cluttered or fussy, it retains a light and airy feel no matter how it is set up.

Design

In this design, absolutely every square centimetre is used for something. The single main space has been designed specifically to function in five ways: as bathroom, kitchen, dining room, living room and bedroom. The only separate space in the apartment consists of a small room for the toilet.

Within the apartment, the wall space is used as the foundation for much of the storage, and nearly everything has been built into the walls in cupboards 60cm (24in) deep. However, this is very subtle and there is little surface detail or evident information as to what is concealed behind the walls. There are no obvious hinges, decorative details or other ornamental flourishes to distract from the flush, sleek finish or to offer any clue as to what is going on behind.

The walls are used as housing for kitchen, clothing and general life-style storage, rather like a giant geometric jigsaw of different shaped squares and oblongs. From floor to ceiling and wall to wall, every possible area is compartmentalised, with spaces and cupboards built in and sized to their assigned function.

The wall space here conceals the apartment's kitchen and units, as well as the only separate space in the small apartment, the toilet, which is hidden behind a panel next to the sink.

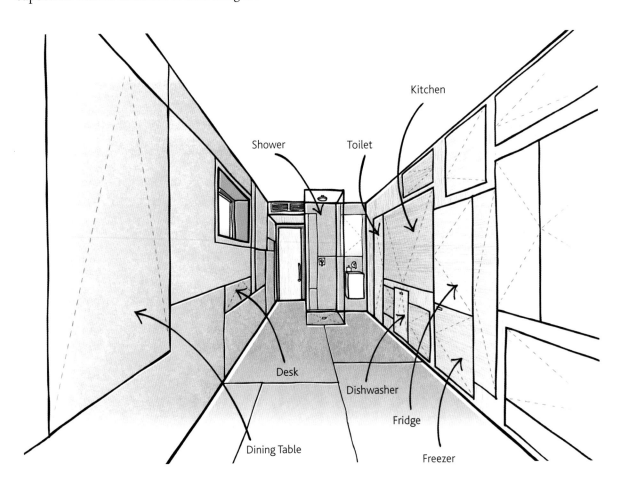

Shower

Toilet

Kitchen

Desk

Dishwasher

Fridge

Dining Table

Freezer

The outside terrace affords spectacular views over the Barcelona skyline, while also providing covert storage for the bed.

AMAZING SPACE ESSENTIALS

1 Remember that keeping everything in its proper place minimises mess and helps prevent bad use of space.

2 Use walls for storage as much as possible, building double walls wherever you can to hide televisions or fold-out tables. What may appear to be a loss of space initially might mean that you gain in the long run as you can shove so much away in the wall systems.

3 Leave the centre of your space free to open up the room and give you space to move things around.

4 It's important to build a good team. Don't be afraid to call in professional help as you will need proper drawings on any major project – it's a worthwhile investment.

5 Think carefully about the essential belongings you have and measure up the space they take up accordingly.

Exterior

The terraced area is raised to facilitate the storage of a slide-out, full-size double bed beneath. There were clear practical restrictions here as the terrace had to be strengthened in order that the roof could hold all the new weight being put on top. Inevitably, all the red tape involved in obtaining the necessary licences and permissions took time, but it was constructed like a proper roof, with its own waterproofing and drainage.

Apart from covertly storing the bed, the terrace now also has an outdoor bath plumbed in. Big enough for two, you can lie back and luxuriate in its warmth, enjoying the distant view of Gaudi's iconic La Sagrada Familia. The steps up to the terrace also function as dining benches and, with the addition of small cushions, when the bed is stowed safely away these are transformed into a sofa.

Despite all the hard-edged functionalism, Christian put a high value on sitting somewhere comfortable, so there are two classic red Tolix chairs on the terrace. Designed in the 1940s, they make an attractive counterpoint to the neutral industrial tones of the wood and concrete, and can be brought inside to use as dining chairs when the table is down.

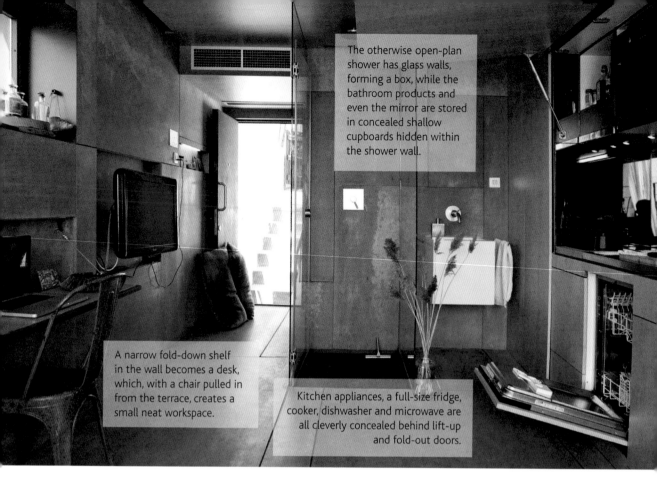

The otherwise open-plan shower has glass walls, forming a box, while the bathroom products and even the mirror are stored in concealed shallow cupboards hidden within the shower wall.

A narrow fold-down shelf in the wall becomes a desk, which, with a chair pulled in from the terrace, creates a small neat workspace.

Kitchen appliances, a full-size fridge, cooker, dishwasher and microwave are all cleverly concealed behind lift-up and fold-out doors.

Techniques

In order to simplify the look of this apartment and create a harmonious space, only two materials and colours were used. The key materials used were wood and concrete, which were chosen for their highly textural and elemental nature. A natural finish was retained on the wood, while the elemental grey of the concrete was left untreated. Any fixings for the doors and windows were made of heavy iron and, for simplicity, internal push/click fastenings were used on the doors.

Most of the wall panels were made of Viroc, a wood chip and concrete mix, and were imported specially from Portugal. As you can imagine, manoeuvring these up the narrow stairs into the apartment was nigh on impossible as they just did not fit. In the end, the only way to get them into the space was to winch them up the exterior of the building, using ropes. Similarly, the shower glass needed six men to winch it up into position – a terrifying experience for all concerned.

The bedside storage resembles simple wooden cubes – lifting their lids reveals the interior storage space. However, even these pull out from beneath the terrace to become long storage units.

GET THE LOOK

SECRET
SPACES

1 When closed, this doorway becomes almost invisible due to the continuity of details and finishes, while the room's bookshelf design trompe l'oeil wallpaper adds an extra layer of distraction.

2 This cupboard office is one space-squeezed home worker. Neat, flush floor to ceiling doors blend with the adjacent wall to entirely close off the space when not in use.

3 Here a minimalist finish is used for this sleek understairs storage space. The finish appears super simple, although the lack of detail conceals the neat, precise workmanship.

WHAT YOU REALISE ABOUT THE CAMPERVAN IS THAT IT'S NOT ONLY A CUTE THING, NOT ONLY A VERY CLEVER USE OF A SMALL SPACE, BUT IT'S ALSO LOVED BY ITS OWNERS. THEY PERSONALISE IT. THEY ADORE IT. I DON'T THINK THERE'S ANYTHING ELSE QUITE LIKE IT.

VW CAMPERVAN

The VW Campervan is one of the most iconic small spaces in the world. Designed to be used as an everyday vehicle as well as a holiday home, it has been manufactured for over 60 years – with different body types and variations – and the very cleverly thought out interior space is all fitted into 4.8m² (16ft²).

A great number of these vehicles were produced, and they lend themselves to renovation, adaptation and customisation. This original spec vehicle is a classic: a near perfect original split-screen 1965 VW Devon Caravette 'Standard' campervan. With its black-and-white checkerboard floor, original curtains and turquoise upholstery, it is a great example of both classic 1960s style and well thought-out design.

THE
BEACH HUT

Beach huts are as traditional a feature of the classic seaside resort as fish and chips and form an enduring part of our architectural and social heritage. Yet usually these tiny buildings are used only during the high days of summer and are left abandoned for the rest of the year to the elements.

After Andy Collett and his partner Emma's honeymoon travel dreams were put to an end due to the impending birth of their daughter, the couple decided to divert their saved funds towards a more humble journey somewhat nearer to home: their own beach hut facing south over flat, sandy Boscombe Beach near Bournemouth. But they wanted this space to do far more for them than the typical beach hut delivers – they dreamt of 'a bolt-hole, a play house, an office and a dining room with the best view in town'. Somewhere for the family to relax and somewhere for their friends to congregate. The journey that it took them on led to something that has changed their lives and relationship with the beach forever.

IF YOU CAN MAKE A SPACE LIKE THIS WORK, YOU CAN MAKE ANYTHING WORK. THIS IS AN INSPIRATIONAL, GENIUS PIECE OF DESIGN.

The Plan

Andy, a yacht designer and his friend Lloydy, a project manager for the Royal National Lifeboat Institute (RNLI), were practical guys who relished a challenge. Neither were qualified craftsmen however, their skills had been learned as boys watching and helping in families who made, fixed and generally re-purposed things, such as the kitchen table or garden shed, in 'make do or mend' mode.

From the start they set themselves a deliberately low re-fit budget for all the materials, fixings and equipment, challenging themselves to come up with ingenious ways of achieving their aims. Their idea was to make maximum use of every square inch by utilising it more than once – there would be no place for waste or slovenly design in this space.

In the three months of planning before they started work, Andy, Emma and Lloydy each wrote a wish list of why and for what purposes they wanted to use the hut, and this formed their brief. They decided they wanted a space to work on their laptops and to sketch out ideas; a traditional beach-front base for their young family where their baby daughter could take an afternoon nap, as well as space for a full-sized dining table and seating for six plus adequate storage. Not content with just functionality, they wanted their hut to be beautiful, too.

Andy also got to know his new neighbours, observing how they used their available space and learning from them the do's and don'ts of seaside DIY. Most of them had installed the usual beach paraphernalia and regular kitchen units, but their diminutive size limited what they could fit in and they were continually moving chairs and other furniture to access things.

AMAZING SPACE ESSENTIALS

1 Always remember that space doesn't have to have a single use – it can be multifunctional. With the beach hut we were able to create five rooms in one.

2 Talk to everyone that will use the space and keep a list of all their requirements in mind.

3 Consider the use of everything within your space very carefully and see if it can be doing more than one thing. Everything in our space had to have at least two uses.

4 Don't over-engineer solutions, the less-is-more principle is magnified in a small space.

5 Don't be bound by convention, keep an open mind!

Design

In an old leather-bound notebook, soon to be known as 'The Beach Hut book', the friends started to sketch; they carried the book everywhere, scribbling down every thought or idea that came to mind. And, as the ideas developed, the whole lot were mocked up life-size in Lloydy's garage using 25ml ply or whatever material was to hand. The footprint was marked up, an old piece of wood was cut to size and positioned, and the configuration of the space began to be planned. As well as drawing out the plan, Andy and Lloydy were keen to test their ideas by walking around the space to ensure that the positioning and scale of each piece of the design truly worked before it was installed in the Beach Hut.

The design didn't happen all at once – it evolved gradually – and, as Andy says, 'Eventually you have a design that doesn't have any problems'.

Construction and materials

The hut is made of pine wood, sealed and painted on the outside and varnished on the inside. A simple panel construction method was used whereby the four walls were each made separately and then fixed to the floor and each other, before the felt covered roof was lowered on and everything bolted together. All the panels are tongue-and-groove, and the hut sits on a base of concrete levelling blocks to raise it off the wet floor and thereby reduce damp ingress.

The limited budget enabled a certain creativity to develop in the choice and acquisition of materials for the interior. The plywood used has been recycled from various projects and was sprayed with car primer before adding the chosen colours, while the fittings were bulk-bought from bankrupt stock.

The water and solar power systems could have been purchased ready-to-go, but instead Andy and Lloydy created their own somewhat ingenious systems. Without a mains water supply, there were two possible solutions: carry a big container backwards and forwards to the tap or create a water system especially for the hut. The water tank is a five-litre dog food dispenser, drilled into, fixings made, hosepipe attached and then fixed to a tap and tiny sink – and hey presto, a self-crafted, working water system on a tight budget. It still needs filling daily but it's a convenient and workable solution.

Tones of soft lime green, grey and duck egg blue on the soft furnishings and cupboard doors help to create a tranquil, relaxed space.

The beach hut has four workable setups.

In setup ❶, The Dining Room, the table is centred in the middle of the room and the six stools are positioned around it.

In setup ❷, The Bedroom, the hinged table has been slid, on a runner, to the side and folded in half. All six stools have been laid on their sides to create the perfect-height day bed for baby Amelia. As they are hollow, the stools function as storage blankets for the cushions, blankets and pillows that are now on the bed.

In setup ❸, The Living Room, five of the stools have been laid together to create a bench, complete with cushions that had been stored inside the stools. The remaining stool is perched next to the table, perfect for sitting and chatting to whoever is on the bench opposite.

In setup ❹, The Office, all bar one of the stools has been stored under the folded table. The remaining stool is positioned in front of the folded table, which now functions as a working desk.

Finishing touches and styling

Andy was realistic when planning the hut – he knew that the limited space would be used intensively and would get battered in the process. Consequently, he thought it best not to make it too shiny in the first place. He was advised by his fellow beach hut owners not to paint the interior as the natural weathering by the sea air would necessitate almost annual re-painting, so alternative finishes and a textural rather than a high-gloss finish were his goals.

It is this marriage of high-end design, manufacture, finish and polish that lifts this project out of the ordinary and into the realms of jaw-dropping creativity and style. The Beach Hut is a neat, graphic, clean-lined space, which is kept grounded by the simplicity and honesty of the choices of materials. However, the execution of the design really does stop many a passerby in their tracks, and they often stop to talk and stare, intrigued by this beautiful, practical and happy little space.

"Introducing multi-functional elements can change the mood of a small space. In lounge mode, the beach hut feels very laid back and totally different to when you are sitting down eating with five other people, while transforming the cooking area into a sleeping area means that within 10 minutes you can be lying back and relaxing."

ANDY COLLETT – OWNER

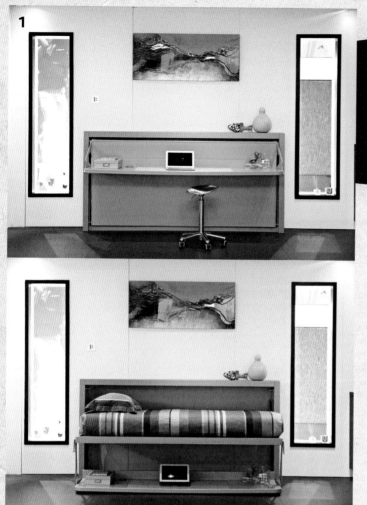

MULTI-FUNCTIONAL STYLE

1 In most foldaway bed designs the bed folds away vertically to the wall when not in use, leaving an empty space. Here the setup cleverly swivels and tilts, so that when the bed is stored away a small desk takes its place.

2 Most foldaway beds pivot through 90 degrees so that they sit vertically within the wall. Here the bed rises on the horizontal so that in its 'closed' position it sits within the ceiling space, revealing the living area underneath. No doubt this is a highly engineered solution, but looking at such examples is helpful in terms of thinking about alternative solutions and looking at all possible available space within a room.

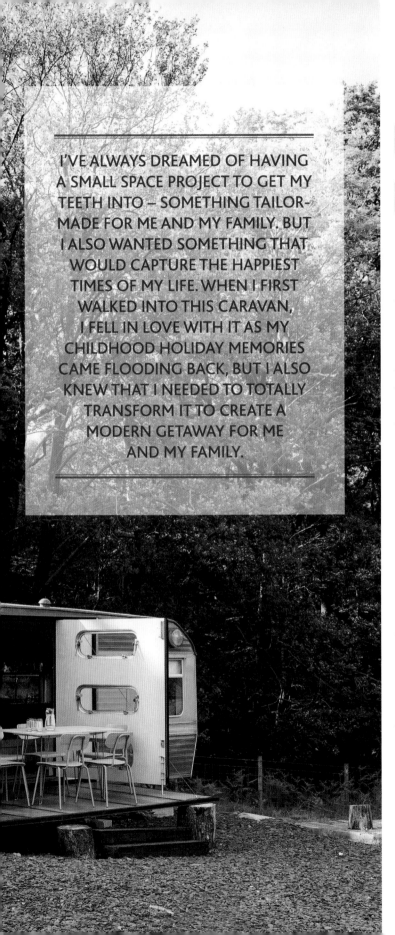

I'VE ALWAYS DREAMED OF HAVING A SMALL SPACE PROJECT TO GET MY TEETH INTO – SOMETHING TAILOR-MADE FOR ME AND MY FAMILY. BUT I ALSO WANTED SOMETHING THAT WOULD CAPTURE THE HAPPIEST TIMES OF MY LIFE. WHEN I FIRST WALKED INTO THIS CARAVAN, I FELL IN LOVE WITH IT AS MY CHILDHOOD HOLIDAY MEMORIES CAME FLOODING BACK, BUT I ALSO KNEW THAT I NEEDED TO TOTALLY TRANSFORM IT TO CREATE A MODERN GETAWAY FOR ME AND MY FAMILY.

George's Caravan

When I was a kid growing up, we couldn't afford to stay in hotels or even B&B's. Holiday life was caravan life, and I absolutely loved it. Caravan holidays were the norm in the 1960s and 1970s, they were an affordable way for families like ours to escape everyday life and have a two-week annual holiday, either by the seaside or in the country. These holidays were great fun and gave us all a wonderful sense of freedom, and even though they didn't cost much money and we didn't do anything spectacular, somehow the happy memories have stayed with me over the years.

While children today are more worldly and accustomed to foreign travel, I had the nagging feeling that I wanted mine to enjoy the simple pleasures just the way I did. But looking at modern caravans left me cold, and it was a real challenge to do something better – I couldn't leave my own design ideals and aesthetic behind. If I were to buy a caravan, I wanted to turn it into something special and to really push the limits of design.

The Plan

My plan was to start off with nothing too finished or fancy but to buy a wreck of a caravan that was super cheap and that we could redesign and restore – putting our own stamp on it. I wanted this to be a project in itself as well as ending up with something amazing: an affordable super-stylish holiday home.

The moment I saw the old caravan I knew it was the one. A 1973 Ace Excellence, it was undoubtedly on its last legs but it had a character all of its own. Most importantly it wasn't trying to look like a fake home, with house-like features; it had its own unique charm and design aesthetic.

From the 1970s onwards, caravans assumed the familiar shape we all know so well today. Instead of being squared off and boxy, they were lozenge shaped, with a gently curved radius on the front and back corners. My caravan was made of the same materials as many others of its day: lightweight aluminium with a timber structure and an awful lot of hardboard. Apart from the three big windows at the back of the seating area, the others were long narrow slit windows, with small metal curved lids over the top – like eyelids.

The design of the interior was typical of a caravan of that period. The materials were chosen for their cost and lightness, and would have been very fashionable in the 1970s. The 'wood' cabinetry and table weren't really wooden at all but wood-effect laminate. Indeed, where any real wood appeared, it was the lightest, cheapest wood possible. The carpets were nylon and the upholstery synthetic velour – both, in their day, highly modern and desirable.

 Even though the finishes were bad, I could still see the possibilities, and the space itself was good, totalling 26.5m² (285ft²). As much as possible was configured within the space. Cranked and slightly awkward angles were used to fit in the kitchen, a fixed dining table and seating area – all perfectly understandable, and an admirable attempt to make the most of the available space and create an open-plan living area.

But one thing struck me immediately: the relationship between this interior and the exterior world was missing … totally. The doorway was narrow and you needed a step to climb in, making it awkward going in and out. Inside and outside were very separate spaces. The only reasonable views and light were from the sitting room windows. This would need a careful rethink as it was really important to me that the whole caravan experience would be all about us, as a family, enjoying and feeling connected with the great outdoors – not stuck indoors behind net curtains.

BEFORE...

BEFORE...

With its curved radius profile and striated aluminium facing, the caravan has a slightly American, slightly futuristic look to it. Over the years, the caravan had been tweaked and slightly modified. I absolutely loved the fake leadlights that had been painstakingly applied to the windows and doors, an attempt to add a bit of Tudor styling to a 1970s caravan. My Dad had done exactly the same to our council house. I was tempted to keep that feature as it made me smile, but, deep down, I knew that it had to go.

Design

William Hardie, a master craftsman and designer, was the person that I chose to work with me on this project. He usually took on more upmarket, grand, bespoke projects utilising only the noblest of materials. He is a highly skilled and creative individual and I knew that if I could persuade him to take this on, we could deal with anything.

However, looking at the old caravan with him was a heart-sinking moment. A common problem with many older caravans is the ingress of damp, and ours was no exception. Although it looked OK at first glance, the slightly musty smell should have rung alarm bells, and when we started to remove the furniture the damp patches were only too visible. Even more worrying was the discovery around the old electric fire of an area of asbestos, which would have to be removed professionally. William's appraisal – the bottom line – was the simple truth and very hard to hear it was, too. Everything would need serious renovation – nothing was spared. The ceiling, walls, floor and undercarriage were all compromised and would have to be reinforced or replaced. Although this was bad news, it only served to galvanise my vision. In every way, the design had

to be radical. We would set about gutting the space, cleaning out the toxic materials, reinforcing the structure and then start again. The work required to drag this caravan into the twenty-first century needed to be radical.

William and I discussed the design at great length, chewing over different ideas and concepts, and eventually two clear strands emerged. The first was the decision to open out the space to deal with the old inside/outside issue. Secondly, we would retain the integrity and original feel of the exterior but would create a completely different world inside. These strands were the starting point for our design.

William's design methods focus on highly creative and imaginative thinking whereby one idea is allowed to develop into another. We considered different ways of opening up the space, from chopping the caravan up into pieces – like a kebab on a stick – to rolling back the roof in the manner of a sardine can, before coming up with the idea to make the entire front wall fold down to become an open deck. I loved this idea, and it addressed both our inspirational themes – in itself, it was a eureka moment of sorts.

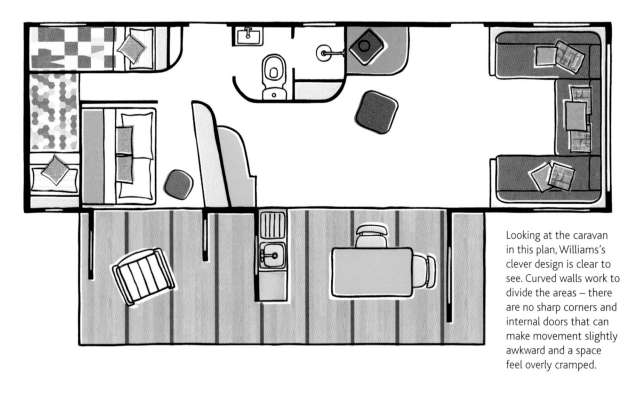

Looking at the caravan in this plan, Williams's clever design is clear to see. Curved walls work to divide the areas – there are no sharp corners and internal doors that can make movement slightly awkward and a space feel overly cramped.

Internally, too, it started to make sense for the caravan to have a north and a south aspect, the 'south' being the opening face. The main bedroom, kitchen and sitting room would all face south and open up to the view, while the bathroom and bunks would face 'north', which was more enclosed, quieter and more private.

The second key design idea was to use the shape of the curve of the roof together with that of the rounded corners of the windows and their 'eyelids' as a key form inside. By using curves in the plywood interior rather than sharp, angular corners we wanted to create a flow to the movement around the caravan. In general terms, this is always a pleasing form – gentle on the eye – and it has an appealing softness to it. We applied this wherever we could, and, coupled with our decision to go with the attractive slightly 1950s look of allowing the end grain of the plywood to show, our themes were taking shape and falling into place.

Materials

Apart from the necessary remedial work, our plan to lower one side to become a deck meant that the rest of the caravan needed reinforcing with a steel beam box frame to make it into a really strong, stable structure.

The other principal material that William and I agreed on was birch-faced ply. This elegant light-toned wood is low key and visually quite soft. Our plan was to use the distinctive end-grain of the plywood throughout the scheme, wherever it was appropriate, such as around the mitres of the windows. In terms of fixings, we decided not to hide them in the usual way of drilling a hole, screwing something in and then filling and sanding. Instead, we used a good product that was visually pleasing – stainless-steel dome-headed screws, in this case – and made them into a feature of the construction.

The ceiling, walls and floor were all insulated. For the flooring, we went the long way round. Using plywood over a

A round, porthole window salvaged from a boat was used to provide light to the bunk bed that sits across the back of the caravan.

Luckily, we were able to site the caravan so that the deck opens onto the Lake District National Park. We couldn't want for a better view.

"THE FOLD-DOWN DECK MAKES THE CARAVAN A FUN PLACE WHERE YOU CAN ENJOY BEING PART OF THE GREAT OUTDOORS – RATHER THAN JUST BEING SOMEWHERE TO SHELTER FROM THE SURROUNDING LANDSCAPE, IT LETS THE CARAVAN WELCOME AND ENGAGE WITH IT."

The gentle lowering of the caravan's exterior wall is deliberately designed to be a jaw-dropping moment. Running on two electric winches from quad bikes, the external doors gently lower to the horizontal. When closed, the seal is weatherproof.

sub-floor of 'eco-floor', we made our own floorboards, cutting them into large rectangles, chamfering the edges and cutting tongue and grooves. Again, we chose specific boards in order to find enough with the same grain. The flooring of the deck had different requirements, however, as it had to withstand the demands of the elements, so we used marine ply instead.

Exterior

The folding-down deck was the first major part of multi-functional design on this project. The external wall lowers by way of winches to become a deck, essentially doubling the floor space of the caravan and opening it up to the landscape and big skies. To provide an alternative to the caravan being either totally open or closed, we fitted large internal doors, which open out from the kitchen/living area, and our bedroom. The doors were fitted with reclaimed narrow boat windows, placed at the appropriate viewing height for adults, children and even the dog.

A curious small space at the end of the bedroom corridor was crying out for something radical. Here we made a fold-down dog and child 'escape hatch', lowered by a simple pulley.

USE OF
SPACE

1 When floor space is restricted an alternate step staircase like this can come in very handy, signficantly reducing the amount of staircase space needed. While it takes a little while to get used to it soon becomes second nature.

2 Mezzanine spaces get put to varying uses, from bedrooms to offices. This one is unusually used as an en-suite bathroom, providing light to the rest of the room by way of a glass balcony.

3 Traditional Japanese houses often use sliding doors as a means of partitioning areas where space is tight. Here the same technique is applied, so the space can be either configured as one open-plan area or as separate living and sleeping rooms.

Interior

The heart of the caravan – and the area which needed the most thought – was the sitting area. This is the most multi-functional space within the caravan and includes my favourite piece of multi-functional furniture – the sofa-bath! The idea for this came about through simply thinking about the available space; the shape and dimensions just worked and there is something fantastically indulgent about lying back in a bath outside. Figuring out how to achieve it in reality, however, was something else. Safety was an important issue and, as the bath needed to be 3m (9ft 10in) from an electrical socket, it was necessary to wheel it out onto the deck. Plumbing too was a challenge. Thankfully William and his team helped me to get it all working.

Another sofa section contains a fold-down full-size wardrobe. This inner plywood structure has a small clothes rail and folds flat to the horizontal. It's a great place to store coats or things you might need if the weather changes. I really wanted these clever multi-functional features to be easy to use, not some bulky, heavy, awkward affair, so William suggested fitting gas struts, like you find in a hatchback car, so that lifting the sofa seat to access what was beneath would be effortless.

The rest of the sofa was the next thing to figure out. In a normal caravan, a slot-out table section would, with a bit of fiddling about, become a bed base, but I didn't want that. I liked the idea of the sofa seats being quite deep, making them really comfortable to lie on or curl up with a book. From this starting point, I wondered whether I could make them into a good-sized bed. That way, if the children's friends or grandparents stayed, we could fit them in without any trouble. William designed a really simple but sleek and millimetre-perfect slide-out bed base. It's so precise that it's incredibly easy and quick to convert the sofa into a giant bed, which is large enough to sleep six children in a row.

Figuring out how not to waste an inch of space when designing the sofa space was a chance for some fun as well as some lateral thinking. Nothing was off limits in the quest to make the space as useful as possible, as these step-by-step photographs revealing the different configurations demonstrate.

The other space that needed a lot of work was the bedroom area. In the original caravan setup there was just one master bedroom sleeping two but, unbelievably – and this never fails to astound me – the area was totally redesigned to configure it to sleep five. Using sleeping areas on different planes and three adult-sized, bunk-style pod-like structures, we found space for my whole family. The natural place for the two traditional vertical bunk beds was on the 'north' wall where there were two of the attractive slit-type windows. It seemed obvious to site the bunks in relation to them. Finding the space for the double bed and the other bunk was achieved by a laborious combination of thinking, sketching, revising and mocking up the space until we landed on a solution that worked. The third bunk has its own little loft area, accessed at the end of the corridor. Using the space above the foot of the double bed, but in its own self-contained pod, this bunk is a real hideaway and has its very own porthole window at its foot, and a recessed shelf unit for books and toys at its head.

Not quite so complicated, but still requiring a bit of thought, were the kitchen and bathroom areas. We decided to sit the kitchen perpendicular to the opening wall on a purpose-built metal frame. This enables the entire kitchen sink unit to rotate through 90 degrees, allowing you to cook or wash up, either inside on cooler days or out in the open on the deck in the form of an outdoor kitchen when it's warm. The retro-styled fridge is built in to the caravan cabinetry, with wall mounted cupboards and open shelves for storage while a two-ring gas hob has been fitted into the surface. The redesigned bathroom is a full-sized shower-room with a small sink and a simple shower fully plumbed into domestic standards – this is not the usual trickle of a shower still found in many caravans.

Styling

I wanted the caravan to be a home from home, which all the family and our pets could enjoy, so nothing could be too precious and all the interior materials had to be durable. Jane, the stylist on this project, had a great approach and was adamant that the interior palette and feel had to work with the Lake District location, with its wooded hills, lush green fields and water. We both thought that the interior should look happy and cheerful as it's a holiday home, while reflecting the colours and tones of the surrounding environment and staying sympathetic to the style of the caravan we were building. I wanted colour but with a clean, crisp feel to it.

The plan came together using the old faithful technique of a moodboard. In fact, it started as three moodboards, each with different ideas, but we eventually focused on one in particular, primarily because of the colour palette. The sofa was upholstered in a graphic 1950s shape, with button details and piping, in an orange (a favourite colour) textured fabric, with

The children's bed area is an ingenious piece of compact design which manages to fit three children's beds into a very small area. The curved lozenge shaped holes in the plywood at the end of the corridor are more than a decorative touch, acting as both the ladder to the bunk bed and also as the door to the 'escape hatch'.

William installed a wood burning stove to heat the caravan, and for the hearth it seemed right, both in the aesthetic and to support local businesses where we could that we sourced some local slate. In terms of the shape, we had it cut to size to use following the same pleasing curve as we had used with the plywood interior. Rather than simply facing in one direction, the curved shape of the wood burner opens it out to the whole living area.

The original but restored 1950s enamel English Rose kitchen units swing out to create either an indoor or outdoor kitchen, and were sourced from a specialist restoration company. A tiny two-gas ringed cooker was set into the top with a white and stainless-steel finish, which provides a touch of simplicity and balances the colour used elsewhere.

the cushions and blinds in a genuine 1960s bark cloth – an abstract tree design, in greens, browns and mustards.

I wanted the children's bedroom areas to have a sense of adventure and informality. We found some vintage knitted and crochet patchwork blankets in antique markets and shops in the local town to William's workshop, and then we appliquéd them with vintage camping pennants purchased from an online auction site. I have very fond memories of my childhood holidays when the bedside bookshelves were well stocked with classic children's books, like Robin Hood and Grimm's Fairy Tales – all great stories for rainy days as well as bedtime – so nearby secondhand book shops were raided, while the only thing left to do was to find some handsome retro and hand-made toys. Again, I wanted them to have a charm without being too precious – a sort of glorified, idealised, magical camping experience for the children.

The main bedroom, with its big windows and doors opening out onto the deck, is a more sophisticated affair. The large doors can swing open, giving the bedroom its own terrace and spacious feeling. The tones are light and fresh, with a modern graphic stylised tree design wallpaper in lime green and white, a simple white textured bedcover and vintage 1960s stool setting the tone. William created some clever storage shelves in the same plywood as the main caravan interior. It is a calm and restful space.

'NOW FINISHED, THE CARAVAN IS ACTUALLY BETTER THAN I EVER IMAGINED IT COULD BE. ALTHOUGH I WAS SO INVOLVED IN THE BUILDING AND DESIGNING OF IT, THINKING ABOUT IT EVERY STEP OF THE WAY, WHAT WILL AND THE WHOLE TEAM HAVE PULLED OFF IS SO CLEVER, SO ELEGANT, IT'S MAGICAL. IT JUST GOES TO SHOW THAT IT DOESN'T MATTER HOW LIMITED YOUR SPACE IS – YOUR IDEAS NEEDN'T BE. IF YOU CAN THINK BIG IN SMALL SPACES, YOU CAN ACHIEVE ABSOLUTELY ANYTHING.'

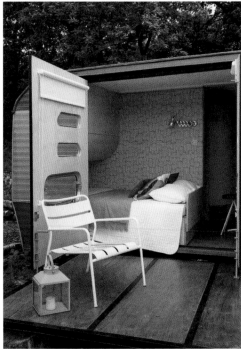

Lozenge shaped recessed shelves in the children's bedrooms repeat the caravan's curved design and give everyone space for their favourite bedtime books and toys. The main bedroom area opens up onto the deck, giving the space a luxurious, spacious feel.

INDOOR
OUTDOOR

1 For an indoor/outdoor space to work well the two areas need to relate to one another. Here the decking and polished concrete are similarly toned and the levels between the two are flush, while the glass doors folds away completely to create one long continuous space.

2 Contemporary furniture and bold colour needn't be confined to an indoor setting. Here an oversized outdoor standard lamp, an orange painted rendered wall and high key colours work well to counterpoint the softer more natural tones of the decking and foliage.

3 This small rooftop terrace repeats the shapes and materials of the indoor space. The circular table inside is echoed ouside, while the deck surface is carried up and repeated over the building's fascia.

RESCUED SPACES

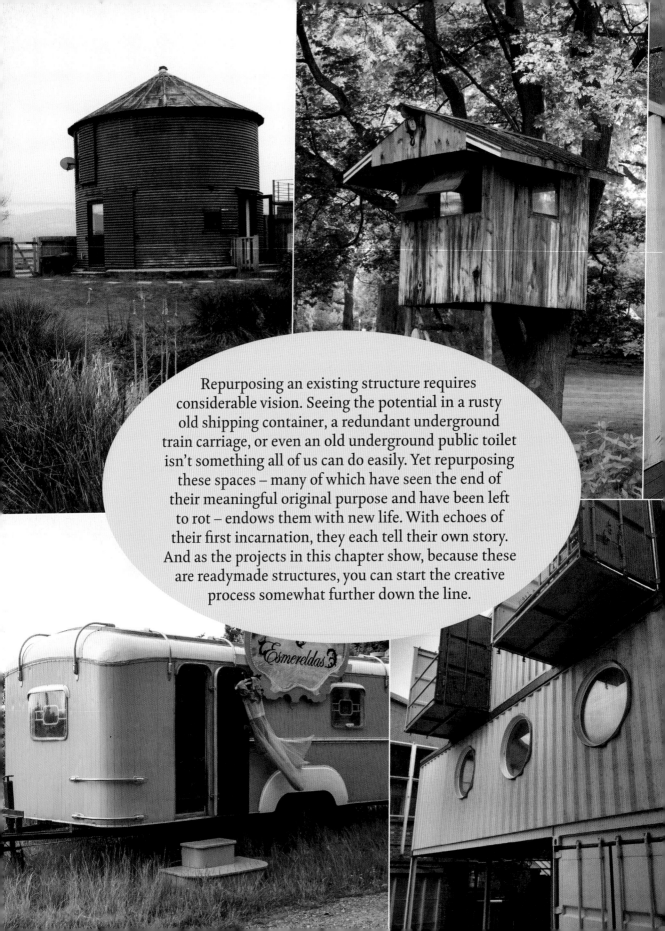

Repurposing an existing structure requires considerable vision. Seeing the potential in a rusty old shipping container, a redundant underground train carriage, or even an old underground public toilet isn't something all of us can do easily. Yet repurposing these spaces – many of which have seen the end of their meaningful original purpose and have been left to rot – endows them with new life. With echoes of their first incarnation, they each tell their own story. And as the projects in this chapter show, because these are readymade structures, you can start the creative process somewhat further down the line.

BEFORE...

THE
UNDERGROUND TOILET

Trying to find an affordable place to live in a big city is a challenge familiar to many of us. Starting out, you have to open your mind to all sorts of possibilities. Yet, while a few home improvements are de rigueur, creating a slick one-bedroom apartment out of a disused underground public toilet is both visionary and extremely brave. This is an incredible example of small-scale city living or, as Laura, the architect and owner describes it: 'It is micro-regeneration – for me, that's about saving sites with an interesting history, which have been abandoned and forgotten'.

Constructed in the 1930s, this dilapidated inner-city public lavatory was not the most obvious place to create a home. For a start, it took nine skip loads of approximately 100 tons of concrete and rubbish just to clear it. The building wasn't listed on the land registry, so even working out who actually owned the space proved a challenge for Laura. This project would test Laura's endurance as well as capture her imagination, and after several years of battling her way through acres of red tape to become the owner of the space, Laura still had the biggest test ahead of her – the job of transforming it into her dream home.

THIS PROJECT PROVES THAT AMAZING SPACES CAN BE FOUND IN THE MOST UNEXPECTED PLACES – EVEN RIGHT IN THE MIDDLE OF CITY LIFE. I CAN'T BELIEVE HOW BRAVE LAURA HAS BEEN TO TAKE ON THIS PROJECT, OR HOW CREATIVE SHE HAS BEEN IN TURNING WHAT WAS A PUBLIC TOILET INTO A COMFORTABLE HOME.

The Plan

The lavatory was built in 1930, during a time of huge civic pride when public buildings were not only made to last but also had a dignity about them – a sense of grandeur not only in their architecture but in their use of materials, too. With its substantial black spear-head railings, impressive cast-iron gates opening onto the pavement and grand balustrades with decorative iron finials, this was not a cheaply built structure. Even the interior was made to last, with tons and tons of concrete and chunky ceramic glazed tiles.

Originally the men's and women's toilets had separate entrances, each via a staircase down from pavement level, and were two totally separate spaces. And, being located eight feet below ground, quite how to turn this unlikely and unpromising space into a liveable home was an undoubted puzzle – with the only natural light coming from the glass pavement bricks above, it's not surprising that the local authority planners questioned whether the level of natural light made the space fit for human habitation.

Laura's solution to the problem was to knock the two spaces together and remove the steps from the women's toilets to create a small outside courtyard garden – the holy grail of city living – and thereby introduce further daylight into the space via a glass door. Additionally, glass windows have been added in the entrance on either side of the front door to channel light from the stairwell into the kitchen and living space. These measures, along with the glass pavement bricks, fill the space with an amazing and unexpected luminosity.

Design

The apartment is essentially an open-plan space with a sitting room, kitchen, bedroom and bathroom. Structurally, there were limits as to how 'open' the space could be. The substantial pillar supporting the pavement above would have been prohibitively expensive to remove, so it has been retained and incorporated into a wardrobe area. The apartment is small but perfectly formed and Laura has found a way of making every inch of space and light work. With the build taking an impressively short five months and a modest budget, her achievements here are not to be underestimated – this is a staggeringly good subterranean home.

Although it is essentially a linear space, with a corridor running the length of the building and the 'rooms' all off to one side, it feels far looser and less structured than this. The area of living space that has been created totals 62m² (667ft²) where previously none existed. Your view flows effortlessly, and focal points, such as the outside garden and hanging chair, have been created to add interest as well as perspective. Indeed, as the space now seems so natural and light you soon forget that you are below ground.

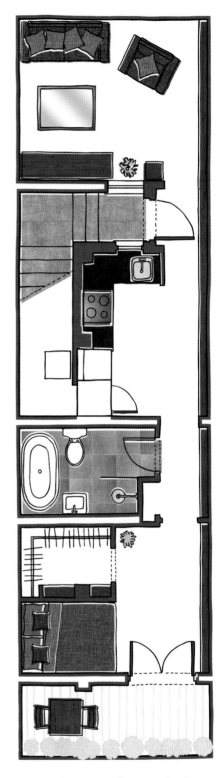

To allow the space to flow, Laura has kept the corridor as wide as possible and avoided internal doors that might otherwise get in the way and leave it feeling boxy.

Finishing touches and styling

Using an almost industrial, functional aesthetic, Laura has retained the essence of the original space, but has gently steered it away from what could have been a clinical, hard-edged look. For example, she has kept some of the narrow brick-shaped, oblong original tiles in the kitchen, using them as a splashback.

Similarly, her choice of flooring throughout the building is dark and richly tonally varied, featuring small wooden blocks of smoked oak parquet. The detailed palette and texture here appeal visually with their subtle detail.

In the same vein, the narrow oak floating shelves lining the length of the building have a form but are by no means regular and give a sense of movement throughout the space. Their use, too, varies according to their location. In the sitting room, they hold books, candles and pictures, whereas in the kitchen section, decoratively placed glasses and spirits function as an impromptu cocktail area next to tidily stacked crockery, hanging pans and neat rows of cooking essentials. The final section of shelving is a joyous and vibrantly coloured image of rows and rows of Laura's shoes, placed at an angle because of the shelf depth and, again, a perfect focal point.

Shelves have been kept narrow to create the maximum display area without sacrificing room space.

This approach embodies the importance of creating visual interest in such a small space. Even Laura's wardrobe has a wall that is plastered from floor to ceiling with a collage of vintage magazine pages, featuring glamorous girls from the 1940s and 1950s. Although the whole space ably manages to be sleek and smart, this is not a minimalist place and there's no shortage of interesting things to look at. Items are carefully rather than randomly placed – neat and tidy – and each one plays a part in relation to its neighbours. Collectively, the individual items form graphic repeat patterns or interesting still lives.

Colour, too, is balanced throughout the space. The palette used is no-nonsense and simple. The materials perform their own work, with rich dark tones in the wood of the floor and shelves, and light-toned walls and tiles in the kitchen. Elsewhere, there is vibrant colour, principally red: textured in the bedroom, luxuriant in the bathroom along with a gold leaf wall, and high gloss in the kitchen.

This is a confident, well thought-out interior with enough self-assurance to allow Laura's character to show through, and it functions effectively as a cohesive, well-designed space.

Rather than using large linear boards, Laura's use of oak parquet blocks helps the space appear more spacious. In the kitchen, although undoubtedly life-worn, the original tiles which gently curve around the corners are redolent with texture and patina.

AMAZING SPACE ESSENTIALS

1 Think about how you will be wanting to move around your space, and try to make it flow.

2 Create a view wherever possible. Everywhere your eye takes you, there should be something worth seeing.

3 In a small open-plan space, think of a cohesive decorating scheme for the entire place rather than tackling it as individual rooms.

4 It's an old trick but high-gloss kitchens really do help a place appear more spacious.

5 Make your plans flexible so that they can change along the way. Laura's initial thoughts were to make this toilet into a café or a mini cinema, but a downturn in the economy and the passage of time led to her making this unusual space into a delightful home instead.

6 Having the practical and professional skills to do the work yourself really does help. As a qualified architect, Laura was able to draw up her own plans and deal with a lot of the submissions. Similarly, on a more practical level, she wasn't frightened of rolling up her sleeves and getting on with the heavy physical work.

This underground home depends largely on borrowed, indirect light. The glass bricks in the ceiling are in fact pavement lights. The deep recesses, painted white, reflect as much light as possible into the space, as does the large floor-standing mirror in the hallway.

"For me, the regeneration of sites like this is such an exciting idea; creating something beautiful and practical carved out of a forgotten space for future generations."

LAURA-JANE CLARK — OWNER & ARCHITECT

1

1 In this living room, light is used as a decorative item. The feature wall adds both texture and tone as well as illumination, creating a beguiling focal point.

2

CLEVER LIGHTING

2 While a tall, narrow staircase can often look oppressive, here the backlighting in the recessed handrail adds a little bit of wow factor, entertaining the eye by leading it up and around the corner.

3 Glass bricks are a popular, reliable way of borrowing light from one room to the next. In this bathroom the glass brick wall makes the most of this 'bonus' light, giving the room a luminous glow.

3

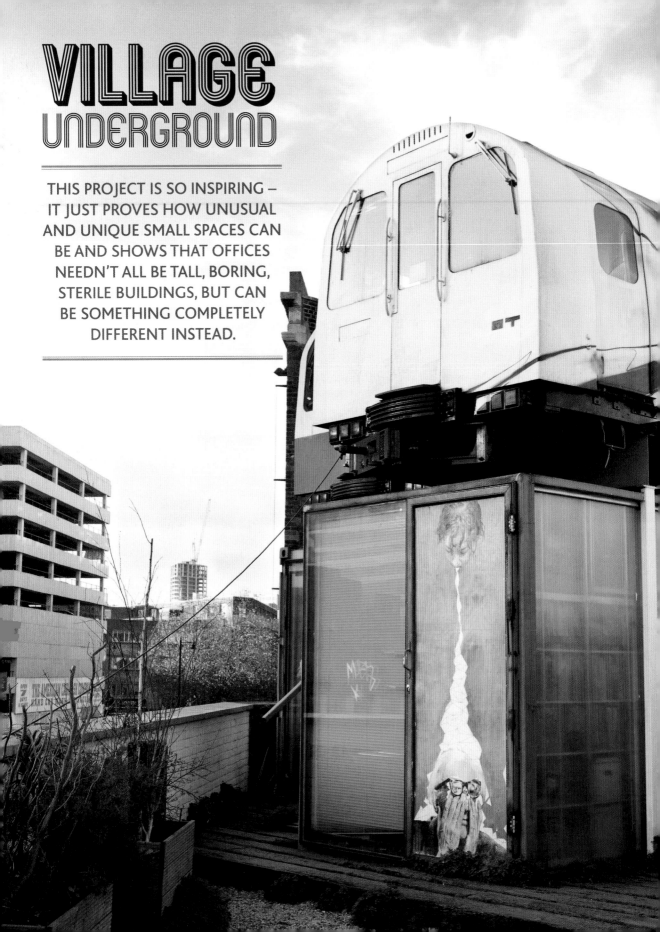

VILLAGE UNDERGROUND

THIS PROJECT IS SO INSPIRING – IT JUST PROVES HOW UNUSUAL AND UNIQUE SMALL SPACES CAN BE AND SHOWS THAT OFFICES NEEDN'T ALL BE TALL, BORING, STERILE BUILDINGS, BUT CAN BE SOMETHING COMPLETELY DIFFERENT INSTEAD.

The lack of affordable desk space in the centre of big cities is nothing new. Sufficient square footage for offices and studios is hard to come by, especially in up-and-coming, hip and trendy locations as well as longstanding financial and business areas.

These four tube train carriages were destined for the scrapyard when Auro Foxcroft, a furniture designer by trade, discovered them. Stuck for office space, he knew that he'd found an unusual and effective way of creating some. Now perched 18m (60ft) up above one of London's main thoroughfares and accommodating 50 people on affordable rentals, Auro has created a visionary and super-hip office with the views to match this project's extraordinary levels of ambition.

The Plan

The overall aim of this project was to establish a creative community with affordable facilities for people starting out on fledgling projects, media, publishing, films and other creative businesses, using decommissioned Underground carriages in a densely urban environment.

Although Village Underground appears to be a totally modern and 'out there' concept, in fact, it isn't a new idea at all – historically, train carriages have been repurposed at different times, albeit not in the last 60 years or so. From the 1920s and 1930s onwards, old train carriages were bought relatively inexpensively and transported to the coast to be converted into holiday homes. Their sturdy construction and existing windows and doors made them easy to adapt and extend, and a quick, affordable way of creating a beach chalet. In addition, after two World Wars, homes were in short supply, so some older railway carriages were taken out of service and utilised as a quick and temporary answer to housing shortages. They were moved to suitable sites and converted into accommodation. Government grants and subsidies were in place to help speed up the supply of suitable plots of land and create 'instant' affordable homes.

Design and logistics

The four iconic London Underground tube carriages used in this build were designed in 1983 for use on the Jubilee line, but suffered from a range of technical problems during their service on the Underground. These included the design and functioning of the motors and generators, together with delays caused by the single opening doors, preventing passengers getting in and out quickly enough at busy times during the rush hour. These problems shortened their service life, and they were 'pensioned off' after only 15 years.

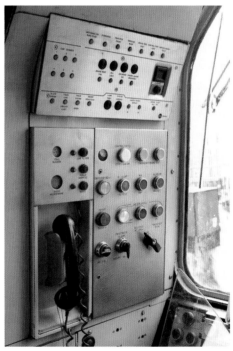

A great piece of functional early 1980s design, the original driver's cab – complete with working intercom – has been left intact. It is used as a meeting room with spectacular high views over the city skyline and busy streets below.

Apart from the seating, many of the original interior features of the carriages – such as the orange door surrounds, the old tube route maps and the hanging passenger straps – have been left intact.

Getting the carriages into place was no mean feat. Their wheels and engines had to be removed in order to make them light and wieldy enough to be transported by truck through the London streets before, in a single 12-hour operation, they were craned up onto the site.

The carriages now sit on top of four shipping containers on what was once a railway viaduct. They have been rewired and replumbed while retaining the look and feel of their original design. As with many of these types of project, the initial purchase was relatively modest, although the subsequent infrastructure, logistics and cranes cost a substantial amount of money. The interiors were modified in order to make them more workable as office space. The original seats were removed and desks built in beneath the windows along the length of the carriages.

This project has to be one of the most unusual and visionary we've seen. It has wit, eccentricity and individualism, and by reusing disused underground carriages, it was relatively inexpensive, too. When you walk down the street, or pass by on a bus, you can't help glancing up at the eye-catching carriages, which have played such a big part in transforming this formerly tired part of the city into the buzzy, creative place that it now is.

LONG NARROW SPACES

1 Rather than try and disguise its dimensions, this principally white and simple hallway embraces its linear nature. A chunky industrial hanging rail sets the tone while wide, long matt bleached recycled wood floorboards guide you down and through the space.

2 Here sheen and finish are often used to make this small space appear less so – creating reflections and bouncing light along the corridor.

3 This narrow kitchen is blessed with a lovely window and terrace. The neutral tones of the thin counter, shelves and units help keep the focus on the spectacular floor-to-ceiling view.

The Shepherd's Hut

THERE'S SOMETHING WONDERFUL ABOUT DEVELOPING AN INTEREST IN SOMETHING NEW AND BECOMING AN EXPERT IN THAT SUBJECT – THE MORE YOU FIND OUT AND LEARN ALONG THE WAY, THE MORE ENGAGED YOU BECOME, OFTEN IN A DELIGHTFUL FASHION. FOR THE OWNER OF THIS SHEPHERD'S HUT, THIS RESTORATION PROJECT WAS SO ABSORBING THAT IT BECAME AN ENJOYABLE OBSESSION.

This shepherd's hut is a great example of an original and sympathetic restoration. The more you learn about buildings like this and their original usage, the more important it is to restore them in a genuine and authentic way. By understanding their provenance, using the correct materials and leaving traces of the human story, we can augment the loving care that past craftsmen have lavished on these structures. Our goal should not be to create something fresh and new but to relish their history and patina.

Rollin, who owns other shepherds' huts in addition to this one, is fascinated by the Victorian era and the Industrial Revolution. He is a naturally practical man and likes to collect vintage tools and classic cars. However, so deep was his love for this original shepherd's hut that his classic Austin Seven car had to go in order for him to buy it. Rollin says, 'I have a reputation for wanting to keep things original. I will not modify them in restoration. It's almost an obsession ... each hut has a personality and tells a story. From the jottings on the wall left by shepherds who have used it to the mouse holes in the walls, I find it all fascinating.'

The Plan

Originally used by shepherds to watch over young lambs or other vulnerable farm stock, these huts provided shelter and a rest space for shepherds while they were working on the land. They were eminently practical spaces and could be towed into the fields along with the animal feed and other essential equipment, such as a small stoves for warming new-born lambs as well as beds for the shepherds, too. While they were on duty, these were their homes.

Rollin Nichols and his wife, both award-winning horticulturalists, saw their first shepherd's hut – a new replica of a traditional hut – at a garden show. His wife liked it and thought it would make an ideal garden room for their home. However, Rollin wanted to source something original with its own character, and set about finding an old hut to restore.

Beginning with some initial internet research, Rollin began to develop a network of contacts, including enthusiasts and specialists, deepening his knowledge and revealing the master designers, creators and craftsmen behind this particular type of build. John Farris, from Shaftesbury in Dorset, was one such builder of shepherds' huts. Rollin found one of his original huts, built circa 1890, and he purchased it from the granddaughter of George Farris (John's brother). Different shepherd's hut manufacturers had their own style, and John Farris huts were distinctive and well built, with their corrugated iron exterior walls, sturdy woodwork, large wheels at the front and smaller ones at the back. They are easily recognisable and are held in high regard.

Materials and techniques

Rollin did all the general restoration work himself, using traditional methods and materials. The manufacturers of shepherds' huts incorporated their own idiosyncratic details, and Rollin wanted to preserve these, too. He studied many other examples of original huts to learn as much as he could about their features, materials and interior layout down to the tiniest details, such as the type of screw fixings used. Thus, when an area of the floor needed replacing he used wood reclaimed from another old hut and deliberately left the repair work visible. Luckily the hut's original small, eye-level sliding window was still in place and functional, and only the original horn panes needed replacing with glass.

The axle, chassis and long bolts that held the two together all needed replacing – 100 years of water dripping off the roof had eventually rotted the ends. This was too specialist a job for Rollin to tackle himself and he had to call in expert help, commissioning a small company that specialised in repairing shepherds' huts. Again, he chose the traditional route to making a new axle and chassis, using locally sourced softwood. The original 'Farris' wheels were restored and reattached, and a new horse shaft made of ash was fixed to the front of the hut. When not in use, this swings upwards and is secured vertically by a catch.

The horsehair that was originally used as insulation in the roof was still in place, so Rollin left this alone. Every other detail was attended to, however, including all the bolts and hinges. The original ones were made individually by a blacksmith and are subtly different from each other. Consequently, they are not standard and Rollin had each necessary replacement made in a similar fashion.

The hut's exterior corrugated iron sheeting with its hard bitumen covering was rubbed down with a wire brush before being primed and painted in traditional paints.

AMAZING SPACE ESSENTIALS

1 Become an expert in your field. Start by using the internet to do your research and develop a network of contacts.

2 Keep your eyes and ears open as you travel about, as word of mouth can often be the best way to go about sourcing a recycled space.

3 Actively build a good reputation as an expert – become someone whom others seek out to get expert advice and opinions. This will attract new leads.

4 Steer clear of buying anything at auction, as these can be expensive places to buy original things.

5 Share what you know with other enthusiasts, and they'll be more likely to share their knowledge with you in return.

A 'tortoise' stove was found to replace the original stove, which had disappeared long ago. Rollin repaired the existing old base with fire concrete, then fitted a flue and applied graphite paste to the stove to restore the finish.

Interior and styling

By looking at a great many hut wrecks, Rollin had learned a lot, and wanted to recreate the same style of bed that he had seen in most of them. These beds are typically simple structures, running across the width of the hut. Underneath them is a slatted front, creating what would have been an area for tending day-old lambs.

In terms of decoration, this hut is a simple, functional working structure. Rollin has set about collecting and, in some cases, has been given some original shepherds' tools and antique agricultural items, such as shears, branding irons, 'docking' tools and even a wonderful old lantern, lit by candles, with beaten horn as a luminescent shade. The atmosphere, although austere in terms of modern comforts or luxury, has its own integrity.

The hut is a comfortable space not only spatially but also in the way it blends into the surrounding environment. With more than adequate ceiling height and pleasing proportions, it is outward looking and warm, and despite the undoubted sheer hard agricultural labour it was built to support and sustain, it still manages to express a kindness and an honest beauty.

The
SHIPPING
CONTAINER

WITH HIS CREATIVITY,
INVENTIVENESS AND
PASSION FOR THIS SHIPPING
CONTAINER, MAX REPRESENTS
EVERYTHING THAT IS
BRILLIANT ABOUT SMALL
SPACE BUILDERS.

> *"I love mistakes – mistakes are healthy in design, as long as you learn from them. They are really important as they show that you have explored avenues and been thinking about what it is you want from your space."*
>
> MAX MCMURDO – OWNER

Despite owning a growing business designing and upcycling objects such as shopping trolleys, bathtubs, engine blocks and washing machine drums into funky modern furniture, Max McMurdo had a problem. His success had resulted in an overflowing workshop, and increasingly he was finding that he needed the space and a quiet environment in order to think and be creative.

A practical person, confident with design, metalwork and professional cutting and welding equipment, Max decided to turn his mind to something out of the ordinary. He was never going to be one for a shed or bungalow made out of wood, instead his small space project would have to be in keeping with what he believed in – and in Max's case that's upcycling with a hefty dollop of mayhem thrown in for good measure. But creating a garden studio out of a repurposed shipping container – and getting the 2 ton, 6 metre hulk of heavy duty steel into place – would test even his ingenuity to its limits.

The Plan

Some years previously, while looking into ways of getting onto the housing ladder in an affordable manner, Max had investigated a wide range of options ranging from narrow boats to caravans, along with the possibility of buying some land and creating a house out of a few shipping containers. Scuppered by finance and planning permission constraints this idea didn't progress, but the research that he did on the matter would now come in handy – the two ideas came together and Max decided to build his garden studio out of one of these ready-made corrugated steel structures.

As Max's business was all about upcycling, it made sense that the container he purchased was one that was nearing the end of its working life. Max found his 6 metre by 2 metre container through one of the many companies selling them on the internet. With its dents, classic red oxide paint colour and

vinyl lettering of the previous owner's livery, Max savoured its obvious history and life well-travelled.

But moving Max's container studio onto site and into its new domestic garden setting – with only a narrow access path down the side of the house – would bring huge problems. Ideally the container would be craned into position. But an awkwardly sited telegraph pole and an underlying listed garage put an end to that idea.

While most people would be defeated by a problem like this, Max relishes a challenge and loves to think around a problem to find a solution. His answer – to cut the container into pieces – came to him initially as a somewhat ludicrous joke, yet having been uttered in jest it seeped in and took root as an idea that might just be worth pursuing. Along with his side-kick and friend Gavin, Max had the skills, knowledge and the equipment needed, and so set about plasma cutting the hefty steel into 20 carefully numbered pieces, carrying them through the narrow passageway and into the garden where they would be re-assembled.

Structure and design

Shipping containers are ideal structures for a re-purposer such as Max. Coming complete with walls, roof and a floor (sometimes lined with high-grade plywood) they are built of heavy duty steel to a series of standard sizes and are hugely robust – designed to be extremely strong and built to withstand the aggressive, harsh environment of exposed long-distance ocean travel. These structural benefits, along with the fact that the proportions are good, the verticals are straight, and the corners are square, mean that fitting out is relatively more straightforward than in a less-formed, more organically shaped structure.

The L-shaped area of recycled decking works as a gentle introduction to the build, and stops it looking too abrupt. It functions both as a practical place for outdoor chairs and furniture and as a transitional space between the garden and the container.

Exterior

The design of the container featured three long sections to be cut into one side of the structure to become windows, with the wide doors at one end to be removed and replaced with glass bi-folding doors. Once the window cuts were made, the cutting for dismantling could begin, meaning that when the container was reconstructed it would not have extra welds in ill-considered places.

Inevitably, putting the container back into one piece didn't run altogether smoothly – in the process of being cut into smaller pieces, the corrugated sections had expanded under the reduced tension and need clamping, tensioning and coaxing back into their original positions. Only once the container was back in its original form could thoughts turn to the interior.

Interior

Initial drawings for the interior had included a small kitchenette and toilet, but once the container was in place and Max was able to walk around it, it became clear that he was trying to squeeze too much into what was a pretty small space. Rethinking things, he decided that the container was now to become one single open space, with the windows onto the garden, and the large glass folding doors bringing more light into the space and visually connecting it to the outside.

Heating for the interior of the container was to be provided by solar panels on the roof, which would itself be planted to both provide insulation and replace the original planting swallowed by the footprint of the container. Once insulated with thermal sheets and clad in panelling, the walls were painted in three shades of grey to reference the corrugated panelling of the exterior. Solutions were kept intentionally simple – the furniture was going to be telling the story in this space.

AMAZING SPACE ESSENTIALS

1 If you are building from scratch, think ahead to how you might eventually use the space so that you can integrate wires, cabling and the like into the build itself. Plastic trunking, ugly cabling and other clutter just says that something is an afterthought.

2 Planning makes perfect. Pull suppliers together and coordinate and plan deliveries right. Draw a timeline of the order that you require things, and make a chart so that you can keep an eye on the project as a whole.

3 Be aware that no design will ever be 100% 'perfect' or as you would dream it to be in an ideal world. Be prepared to make compromises to meet your budget.

4 Where possible work with standard components. Say to yourself and suppliers, 'this is roughly what I am after ... is there a way that I can achieve this using stock items?'. You may need to tweak and adjust your plans in order to make this happen.

5 If you are building your home, never forget that this is one of the only places in life where, whatever job you do or hobbies you have, you can be creative and expressive yourself. Don't waste that opportunity!

Finishing touches and styling

To finish the container – and because the space is to be used as a showroom as well as a design office – Max has moved in samples of his furniture. The pieces included are not simply on display, they are functional too. A pair of bathtub chairs for instance are placed in a conversation pattern so that they can be useful for meetings.

All this recycled furniture has a story and demands consideration. The stereo speakers that sit on the deck are actually upcycled petrol cans, the side table is an old engine, and yes, you really can sit in that old shopping trolley. As there is more to this furniture than first meets the eye, Max has deliberately left space around these pieces to allow them to be considered in detail.

In the spirit of reusing, one section of the corrugated panel that was removed to form the windows has became a table top, resting on trestle legs with a glass top to provide a flat surface. The other two sections have sculptural properties and are propped up as decorative panels against the tall brick wall at the back of the decking.

To finish the container, Max designed an awning that utilises the lifting points which would have originally been used to crane the container into position. Made by a sailmaker this simple, elegant feature acts not only as a practical sun shade but also helps to soften the rigid lines of the container, cleverly working along with the decking to embed the building into its environment.

The container's original lifting points are now used as fixing points for carabineers to tension and fix the triangular-shaped awning.

METAL
RECYCLING

1 A sliding wall of worn, heavily rusted metal adds texture and decorative element to this space, as well as acting as a counterpoint to the clean modern lines of the lampshade, table and chairs.

2 Old corrugated iron is a seriously tough and hard-working look, but one that can add a great deal of atmosphere – bringing with it its affiliation to the agricultural outdoors,   and industrial landscapes.

3 The large scale of the industrial ducting and its crisp metal finish is set in contrast here to the soft toned walls and aged wood beams, sharpening up this kitchen's otherwise rustic feel.

Esmerelda's
EMPORIUM OF
Vanity

THIS BOUTIQUE
BUSINESS IS A
DELIGHTFUL AND
VERY MODERN
REINVENTION OF A
CLASSIC CARAVAN
FOR WHOM
CUSTOMISATION IS
NOTHING NEW.

For a simple but effective transformation, Esme reupholstered the chair seat pads with attractive fabric and a heavy-duty staple gun.

To many people an old caravan is just that ... an old caravan and nothing more. But for the knowledgeable, the Coventry Knight is an iconic and legendary piece of caravan history. Monumentally expensive when new, costing more than a small house, and designed using what were then groundbreaking materials, it was the prestige caravan of its day. Originally made of steel, its sturdiness and distinctive shape, with gently curved corners, a curved tubular trim and windows, makes it easily recognisable – these were sturdy beasts, built to last.

For Esme Worrel, a lover of aniquities, vintage and beauty in many guises, the chance spotting of a dilapidated Coventry Knight was just the jolt she needed to kick-start a new business idea. Growing up in a traditional horse-drawn gypsy wagon and then having moved to a vintage caravan of her own, Esme had nothing but positive memories of caravan life and she could see in this caravan the opportunity to create an exciting business project of her own, 'Esmerelda's Emporium of Vanity' – a mobile, vintage beauty parlour which could be taken to weddings and festivals. But getting this rusting beast into shape and ready for purpose on a limited budget would test Esme's optimism to its limits!

The Plan

With their deluxe design, decorative flourishes and flamboyant appearance, Coventry Knight caravans have always had an intrinsic appeal. As well as being status symbols and beloved of the travelling communities, they were functional and used as business vehicles by banks, building societies and dentists to access rural communities, albeit in bespoke designed, specially fitted-out versions.

This particular caravan was in a sorry state when Esme discovered it – it was literally falling apart. The chassis had entirely rotted through and needed replacing, the roof was full of holes and it had no wheels, but she could see that this was a unique opportunity to own one of the classics of British caravan history, and it was her commitment to restoring the caravan that persuaded the original owner to sell it to her. Esme's plan was to repair, renovate and transform the caravan from this skeleton into a stylish, luxurious and charming, yet practical space for her beauty business, which would trade heavily on its vintage style.

Esme's partner built the sturdy, curved steps up to the front door and painted them the same colour as the caravan to create an elegant, quietly dramatic, entrance.

Exterior

Over the years, the caravan's exterior had been repainted many times, and there were so many layers of paint that figuring out the original colour wasn't easy. Esme followed her instincts here and eventually decided on a pale blue. It not only reminded her of seaside holidays but it also had a vintage feel that was fresh and clean looking.

The original design includes translucent acrylic curved coving, which runs around the entire top edge of the caravan between the walls and the roof. This, along with the three roof lights, adds considerable light to the interior but, understandably, the coving becomes fragile over time and the acrylic in the roof lights had to be replaced. Even the structure of the roof needed work done, and additional wooden structural supports were added to the interior.

Interior and styling

Esme knew that the star of the show had to be the caravan itself and that the interior colours needed to be subtle and natural so as not to overwhelm the external design. Stylistically, she took her direction from the materials used in the caravan, especially the wood interior. She describes this as an intuitive process, and even the furniture she acquired was serendipitous. The caravan restoration took place in a warehouse facility that also housed a furniture storage company, so if any pieces were no longer wanted by their owners, they were offered to Esme on a first refusal basis. If the item wasn't the right period or style, she considered how she might

customise it – by painting using cans of spray graffiti paint and then ageing it or by rubbing it back to create a distressed finish. The floorboards were replaced with pine boards before being waxed.

Esme's general approach to styling is based on her inherent dislike of new things. Genuine vintage is always preferred and, although she is not a slavish believer in recycling, it's her natural choice whenever possible. The caravan has a stately feeling – spacious and roomy. The furniture – dressing table, chest of drawers and stools – is full sized, and, although much of it was made in the 1980s, it has classic details and decorations, such as scrolls, swags, and ball and claw feet which lend themselves to vintage reinvention.

Long benches line the walls, ready for customers and also to accommodate newly glammed-up girls waiting for their friends to finish their treatments. The atmosphere is lady-like but fun, and there's a big sense of enjoying yourself and making an effort – that scruffiness isn't appropriate. These signs of gentility are reflected in the bone china tea cups, perfume bottles, music scores, hair pins, handbags and accessories, along with large jars of glitter and false eyelashes. There is no option here but to join in, look suitably drop dead gorgeous and have some fun.

"The Emporium of Vanity has been the result of a lot of passion and dedication, but I have loved the challenges that the restoration and redesign of the space have presented." ESME WORREL – OWNER

AMAZING SPACE ESSENTIALS

1 Use repurposed and revitalised items, to give your space a strong identity and a retro or vintage feel without breaking the bank.

2 Be prepared to learn how to use new tools and acquire new skills and expertise. Utilise the resources to hand, including DIY books and online video tutorials.

3 Don't be afraid to ask friends and family for help. If you supply good food and drink and throw a decorating or DIY party, everybody will have a ball. People like to take part in an exciting project.

4 Become a savvy shopper: can you get carpet off-cuts for a small space or the last couple of reduced rolls of fancy wallpaper? Shop around, make enquiries and ask what's available. Spending less does not necessarily mean compromising on quality or integrity.

5 Spray paint can be a blessing for achieving a neat paint finish on revamped furniture. It can be nerve-wracking transforming objects but this method gives a really professional finish and it's simple and cheap, just be sure to shop around and research which brands are easiest to apply.

6 It is important not to compromise your vision too much. Make sure you know when to spend money and where it is safe to save the pennies. A few well-placed features can make all the difference to a space, and some clever shortcuts will always go unnoticed.

7 Don't scrimp on the essentials, such as floors, structure and other integral features – it's not worth it. If tackled well, they should only need doing once and will add value to your space.

8 Nothing makes a space more inviting than the personal stamp of its creator. Especially where expense has been spared, using a few key items, such as pictures, can give your place a unique edge that is hard to replicate.

NEW SPACES

This chapter looks at creating new spaces in places that, although they may not be immediately obvious, are evident if you look closely enough – the space on the roof, the awkward piece of agricultural land, the space between the ground and the tree canopy, even the forgotten, grotty corner of your backyard where it's hard to grow anything. These invisible, overlooked or forgotten spaces that exist in both urban and rural environments afford exciting opportunites, as the inspirational projects featured here show.

THE EXBURY EGG

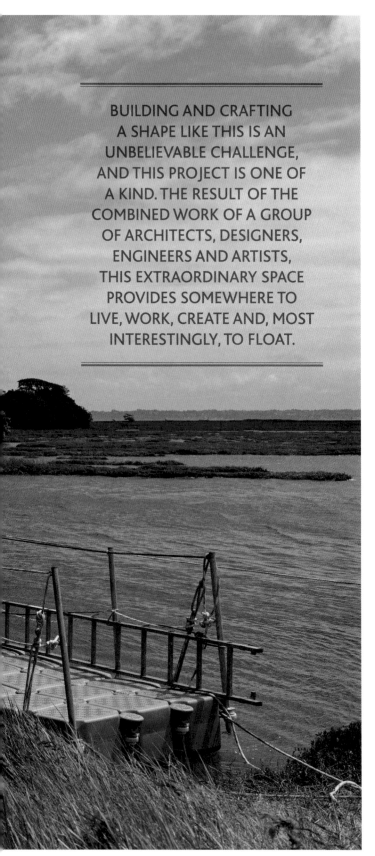

BUILDING AND CRAFTING A SHAPE LIKE THIS IS AN UNBELIEVABLE CHALLENGE, AND THIS PROJECT IS ONE OF A KIND. THE RESULT OF THE COMBINED WORK OF A GROUP OF ARCHITECTS, DESIGNERS, ENGINEERS AND ARTISTS, THIS EXTRAORDINARY SPACE PROVIDES SOMEWHERE TO LIVE, WORK, CREATE AND, MOST INTERESTINGLY, TO FLOAT.

The egg is such an everyday shape that we hardly ever stop to think about it, but in design and architectural terms it is a very complex structure. This egg, undoubtedly, is a technically challenging project: a hybrid of the different worlds of art, science and architecture. Anchored like a boat to the bed of the Beaulieu River in Hampshire, England, this large, wooden structure floats with its lower part concealed below the waterline as it rises and falls with the tides.

With its surreal, exaggerated nature, this unique build wouldn't look out of place in an art-house or sci-fi movie, as part of an art installation or even some bizarre scientific experiment. As it is, the egg manages to capture elements of all the above, while also being a thing of exceptional beauty.

The Plan

Located within the watery landscape of a tidal river estuary, this project set off with a multi-disciplinary approach right from the start. The brief given to a team of architects, engineers and artists was to design a temporary, low-tech, off-grid, sustainable space that would provide artist Stephen Turner with somewhere to live and work for a year. It would need to be sympathetic to its environment and, just to make things a little bit more tricky, its final location would be a sensitive conservation area.

As the artist in residence, Stephen would use the egg to observe this fascinating, daily-changing environment up close, studying the water's edge between high and low tides and observing the landscape closely for effects of global warming and tidal erosion. The pod itself was to become part of the environment, weathering with the elements as the year progressed, and engaging with the micro-environment and flora and fauna of the water.

As the materials and techniques used needed careful selection involving a creative and practical collaboration between the disciplines of architecture, art, engineering and design, the complicated and challenging design brief was given to a local firm of seasoned boatbuilding craftsmen experienced with both modern and age-old construction methods. The plan was to design the egg so that it would function like a bird hide, camouflaging the occupier from the natural wildlife in order to observe it in a quiet and non-threatening way.

Design, structure and materials

Measuring 6 x 3m (20 x 10ft) and anchored to the riverbed, the egg is designed to move up and down with the tides. Solar power is harnessed as the energy source with the project following the principles of 'lean, green and clean' and 'reduce, reuse and recycle'.

The egg was not destined to become a sleek luxurious recreational space; instead, it had to be fitted out with the bare essentials that Stephen needed to live a modest, simple life – a bed, a stove, a desk and a wet room, with enough power for his laptop, mobile phone and digital camera.

Exterior

The exterior of the egg was clad in cedar wood, as much of which as possible recycled or reused from old shed and garage doors. For the egg to be watertight and have a natural unfinished wooden exterior – so the effects of weathering and erosion would be visible – the cedar was double layered, with a layer of glass epoxy placed in between to create a waterproof membrane.

Various solutions were worked through to enable the egg to rise and fall with the tides while staying upright and stable without rotating. Planning restrictions meant that posts couldn't be fitted into the river bed, but a solution emerged. Two weighted fins were applied to the egg, like the twin keel on a boat, to stop any possible rotational movement.

A large circular window in the top of the egg acts as the main light source, while affording fabulous views of the clouds scooting by in the coastal winds.

Construction and interior

Constructing this complex 3-D shape out of 2-D materials presented yet more creative and practical challenges for the team. Eventually, they opted for a design that mirrors the way in which a roof is constructed, with battens fitted on top of the trusses and a covering over the top. However, although the egg follows basically the same form, albeit in a curved shape and principally in wood, it was made in two halves and then assembled together.

The simple interior echoes the ethics and principles of the exterior. Inside the main studio room there is a kitchen area with a two ringed gas stove to cook on, and a tiny sink. On the opposite wall is a desk area for writing, drawing and sketching with a simple stool. The small marine charcoal-burning stove the egg houses was manufactured nearby, and the charcoal that Stephen uses for drawing as well as fuel is made from Spartina grass, which is grown locally.

For Stephen, the importance of this ethical relationship with nature cannot be overstated and reflects the aim of this project as a whole, which succeeds in the task of raising awareness of this very special salt marsh location, while treading as lightly as possible upon this spectacular, and fast-changing landscape.

Although spartan, the interior walls are made of the same narrow wooden slats that form the egg's exterior – the detailed repetitive texture helping to create a sense of warmth and envelopment.

Two large door hatches open up on either side of the main studio room, connecting the interior space with the outside elements.

THE HUT ON THE ROOF

In any major capital city, space is at a premium, and finding a way to expand and create new living areas requires ingenuity and imagination. Yet despite what many believe, you really don't have to restrict yourself to building solely on your existing 'footprint'.

Building on rooftops is an effective solution to the problem of how to extend an existing space and create additional rooms. Usually, the style of the house is continued upwards, and strenuous efforts are made to visually blend the new-build extra floor with the building below. Here, however, the owner has created a unique hideaway – slap bang in the centre of one of the world's busiest cities – with a totally different style and mood to the rest of the house below. When you ascend the staircase and enter the hut, it's a bit like going on holiday. It's a supremely creative and inspiring space that is both stylish and welcoming.

I ABSOLUTELY LOVE THIS PROJECT, BECAUSE WHAT IT SHOWS IS THAT EVEN ON TOP OF THE MOST DIFFICULT BUILDING RIGHT IN THE MIDDLE OF THE CITY, WITH ALL THE PLANNING CONSTRAINTS IN THE WORLD, YOU CAN STILL CREATE THE MOST PERFECT SMALL SPACE RETREAT.

The outside of the building's, rough, wavy edged, highly textural sawn oak creates an arresting contrast to the interior's warm-toned cherry wood veneer.

The plan

This house stands in the centre of the City of London in an area that was formerly dedicated to light industry and watch-making, but which has subsequently evolved over several decades into a buzzing artistic quarter. The idea here was to create a new kitchen on top of the narrow roof space, but this was to be far more ambitious than just a single room – the talented and successful graphic designer who owned the house wanted it to have a spirit all of its own as well as being a retreat in which she could cook, entertain and relax. She didn't want to follow the well-trodden path of a slick modern box-type extension; she wanted something much more exciting and individual. Her vision was a hut on the roof, constructed in wood, with a small outside terrace for enjoying the warm summer evenings.

City planners often hold strong opinions about what is permissible, and the planning application here was simply for a single-storey extension on top of a four-storey house. Permission was eventually granted but on the proviso that it would not be visible from street level. The answer was to position the structure inwards from the facade of the building behind a small north-facing balcony.

Planning authority regulations required the hut to be invisible from street level. Setting the frontage back meant that a small but worthwhile amount of space was available for use as a terrace.

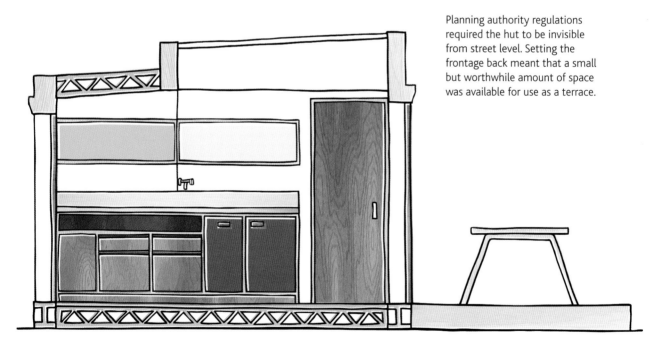

Design and construction

According to the project architect Scott Batty, people are 'more expressive' when extensions are located on rooftops, out of sight from down below. Setting them back from the roofline gives you the freedom to do something more personal and out of the ordinary – something individual, with its own character and style, independent of the building. And given this is a narrow street with relatively tall buildings, the extension did not have to be set back too far.

The external construction Scott designed is a rough-sawn oak box that sits on top of the building. Some 15m (50ft) up, it soon earned itself the name of 'the hut on the roof'.

Measuring 1.1m² (12ft²), it is accessed by a tall, narrow staircase. As you reach the upper floor, the interior wall of the staircase is lined with the same sawn oak as the exterior, giving you a clue as to the style and feel of what is to come. The hut itself comprises of a kitchen with a wood burning stove and a small dining area – it is, essentially, a hideaway, which has a different feel to the rest of the house. The spectacular feature is a retractable glass roof, which slides open to the starry night sky or sunshine. This is no dingy cabin but is instead a light, bright, modern and well-ventilated space.

The original plan was to build the 'hut' off-site and then crane it into position on top of the building. However, this proved too costly an option, and therefore it was built in situ. Insulated with sheep's wool and kitted out with solar panels, this is a rustic retreat with a very modern edge and contemporary approach to energy conservation.

Aesthetics, materials and finishes

There is a growing interest in the warmth of 'hut-like' structures – for simple buildings that are in tune with natural materials, creating highly textured and comforting living spaces. In both their design and simplicity, they provide a restful retreat from the busy and complicated nature of modern life. They illustrate a focusing and simplification of thought, and have a built-in contemplative aesthetic. This trend goes way beyond architecture, reaching out into interiors, music and fashion, too.

Reflecting this, the qualities of all the materials used in this build were considered very carefully. As a contrast to the rough, wavy-edged, highly textural sawn oak on the exterior, the interior is lined with a lovely warm-toned cherry veneer, giving it a much sleeker and more highly finished look. With a modern wood burning stove, stainless-steel work surface and sink, open box-style shelves and big glass doors opening out onto the terrace, it is a clever and stylish way to create more living space – luminous and rustic without compromising comfort or luxury.

The retractable glass roof and doors to both ends of the hut mean that on summer evenings the space can be opened up and connected to the elements.

AMAZING SPACE ESSENTIALS

1 If you are planning a structure on a roof space make sure that you have sought professional advice. Structural loading will be an issue, and approval from the relevant planning authorities will be needed.

2 Think carefully about the materials you are planning on using. Although the conventional approach when building in a densely populated space is to keep things in line with the surrounding buildings, heading off in a different direction altogether sometimes works well too.

3 Remember that sometimes planning restrictions can help alternative creative solutions emerge. In the case of The Hut on the Roof, a small terrace was only included in the design to accomodate the need for the building to be set back from the eyeline of the street.

4 Don't forget to take into account access for equipment and materials. Narrow doorways and stairways with tight turns and entranceways affect materials and goods access in and out and will need consideration.

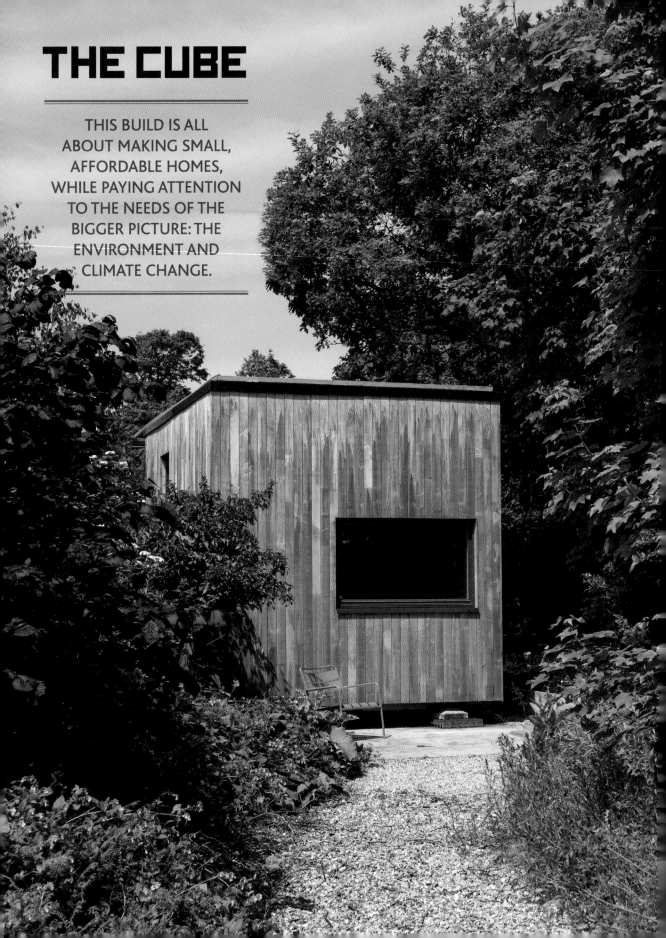

THE CUBE

THIS BUILD IS ALL
ABOUT MAKING SMALL,
AFFORDABLE HOMES,
WHILE PAYING ATTENTION
TO THE NEEDS OF THE
BIGGER PICTURE: THE
ENVIRONMENT AND
CLIMATE CHANGE.

Sometimes we need to see examples of how good our living spaces could be in order to realise how very complicated and inefficient they often actually are. Here, in this compact space, considerable thought has gone into planning every single feature, creating an efficient solution for the provision of quickly built housing in times of need. It also illustrates how we could live in a more sustainable way. The aim of this project is to create affordable, movable, reusable and, ultimately, recyclable homes, and in so doing its creator hopes to inspire more environmentally friendly builds.

Conceived by Dr Mike Page, engineer and professor of Cognitive Psychology at the University of Hertfordshire, The Cube attempts to tackle the thorny issue of climate change and how it can be addressed by the house building of the future. This innovative compact home sets out a new design for low-carbon living, demonstrating how one person can live a comfortable, modern existence with minimal impact on the environment.

The Plan

This project was inspired by Dr Page's desire to help people cut their carbon emissions. Although the technologies exist for low-impact living, he believes there are psychological reasons why people are slow in applying them to their own lives and thought that providing a practical example of how this can be done, using modern construction and fitting-out techniques, is preferable to just talking about it as an idea.

The original inspiration for this project was a smaller cube building produced in the 1990s by Munich University and using fold-out beds and other traditional space-saving concepts. However, Dr Page wanted to produce a compact, movable living space that was more homely – without having to fold up and put away furniture – but still showcasing the potential of small-space dwelling and multi-functional living.

The cube is an entirely open-plan space. Spacially the design is very clever – avoiding the sense of being overly cramped while managing to feel simultaneously light and comfortable.

Design

Measuring 3 x 4 x 3m (10 x 13 x 10ft) internally, the Cube contains a small double bed, a bathroom, a four-seater table and three-seater sofa (although not both at the same time), and a kitchen, including all the usual equipment. Made using sustainable materials, its 36m³ provide everything a single person or couple might need.

The space was designed in a manner that would allow it to be classified as a 'static caravan', so it could be transported on British roads without an escort. Another important design consideration was that none of the techniques or technologies used within the Cube should be applicable solely to small spaces – Dr Page wanted everything to be able to be scaled up appropriately, so that anything featured within the Cube could be utilised in homes and businesses of all shapes and sizes.

Exterior

The building, now in its second version, is supplied as a kit which, like flat-pack furniture, can be assembled easily with minimal tools – in this case, three: a spanner, rubber hammer and screwdriver.

The Cube's exterior is clad in sustainably forested sweet chestnut wood, and even the foundations do not escape the eco scrutiny and detailed thought that is evident throughout the design of this unique building. They use considerably less concrete than traditional building methods employ and are both reusable and recyclable as well as being designed to leave no lasting imprint when removed. Similarly, the building is fixed to the ground with earth anchors, each of which is capable of resisting over a ton of pull-out force but can be removed simply by unscrewing.

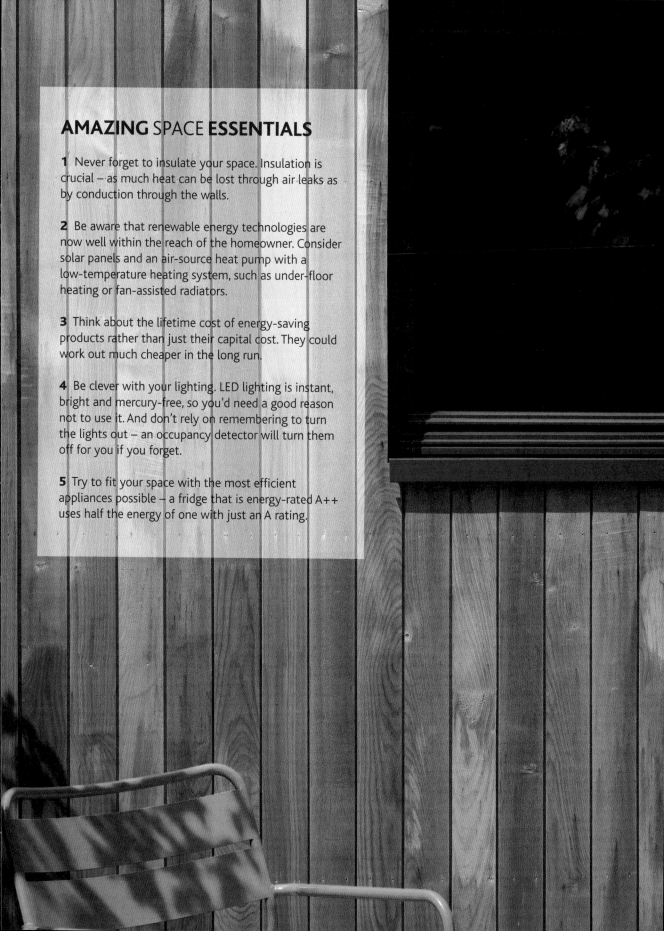

AMAZING SPACE ESSENTIALS

1 Never forget to insulate your space. Insulation is crucial – as much heat can be lost through air leaks as by conduction through the walls.

2 Be aware that renewable energy technologies are now well within the reach of the homeowner. Consider solar panels and an air-source heat pump with a low-temperature heating system, such as under-floor heating or fan-assisted radiators.

3 Think about the lifetime cost of energy-saving products rather than just their capital cost. They could work out much cheaper in the long run.

4 Be clever with your lighting. LED lighting is instant, bright and mercury-free, so you'd need a good reason not to use it. And don't rely on remembering to turn the lights out – an occupancy detector will turn them off for you if you forget.

5 Try to fit your space with the most efficient appliances possible – a fridge that is energy-rated A++ uses half the energy of one with just an A rating.

The Cube is a well-insulated building, with 140mm (5.5in) insulation in the walls and 120mm (4.7in) in the floor. The glass used in the windows is triple glazed. Using solar photovoltaic panels, the building is designed to generate as much energy as it uses over the course of a year. The only connections it requires are to the electrical grid and a source of cold water – no mains drainage is required as waste is either composted or processed on-site by a small reed bed and soak-away.

Interior

A simple integrated layout allows every inch of vertical space, as well as floor space, to be used. This ingenious design uses many of the space saving elements seen in the other projects featured in this book, but here they are coupled with some serious eco credentials and easy and affordable assembly to create a seriously impressive package.

Essentially, the space is formed of three internal levels, the ground floor consists of a seating area and dining/work table, the middle level the shower, bathroom and kitchen, while the upper area houses the bed space. All three levels are open plan, and the staircases between them are comprised of short alternate boxed cube steps. Although these take a little getting used to, the movement between the spaces and levels is surprisingly comfortable, easy and thought out. The flow works.

The negative spaces between the levels, and within the staircases are used for storage, both in terms of cupboards and shelving space, and along the length of the bed there are deep recessed shelves for storing clothes and books. This isn't a space that is all form – the storage provided is both sizeable and practical.

The cube's hot water supply is stored in a 100-litre pressurised cylinder, which is designed to fit under the shower, and the space is warmed by an air-source heat pump. Water use is minimised by the installation of low-flow, high-performance showers and taps. There is a low-energy LED lighting system, while even the TV, kitchen appliances, cooker, fridge and washing machine are eco-friendly, low-energy models.

As over 90 per cent of the energy associated with water use is used in heating cold water, the Cube is fitted with low-flow taps and a low-flow (aerated) shower head, which make a significant difference in reducing usage.

Fixed to the wall with runners the dining table can slide into the corner and become a desk. The upholstered lids of grey stools beneath lift up and the interior of the stool itself can be used for storage.

Materials and finishes

Internally, the Cube is lined with birch plywood. The finishes are clean-cut and simple – with charcoal and pale grey matt fabrics on the sofa and footstools, and a shiny red gloss on the kitchen units – enabling owners to create whatever style of living space they desire.

Essentially, this is a very clever, low-cost, sustainable open plan home, a condensed space that is ready to move into. It's an inspiring example to those us who live life on a larger scale of how we could import these eco principles and design features into our own homes, whatever their size or location.

Hollow alternate cube steps take up less space than a conventional staircase and are used as additional storage.

Long deep shelves, used for storing clothes, run the length of the bed – their staggered shape mirroring that of the stairs.

THE
SCHOFFICE

When most of us plan a garden office, we tend to look at images of off-the-peg structures that come delivered as flat packs, or we follow a readymade format designed to suit as many people as possible. However, this is something else – an architect-designed garden office with a sweeping deck and the large curved form of an ocean wave.

It is hard to believe that this amazing building was prefabricated in a workshop as a kit – but doing so allowed for precise construction, speedy onsite erection and minimal disruption for the owners. Structurally lightweight, both the interior and exterior are clad in slim strips of white oak that have been steam bent into the complex elliptical shape. The wooden canopy is part-filled by an enclosed glass studio and, around the back, there's some handy garden storage. One long narrow skylight runs above the desk in the glazed section while the other is open to the sky outside in the open part of the ellipse. With its enchanting sculptural form, this office is not only beautifully designed, it's also beautiful to look at, too.

A QUIET PLACE TO WORK AT THE BOTTOM OF THE GARDEN IS THE DREAM FOR LOTS OF PEOPLE. BUT RARELY DO THOSE DREAMS TEND TO END UP LOOKING QUITE THIS BEAUTIFUL.

THE
Tree Tent

THIS INNOVATIVE DESIGN
IS A BEAUTIFUL BLEND OF
PRECISION ENGINEERING
AND ANCIENT
WOODWORK SKILLS.

A chance encounter with a newspaper feature proved to be the inspiration behind this project for mechanical and architectural engineer and designer Jason Thurley. The wooden structures that he read about – spherical tree-houses rigged into the Canadian woodland – fired his imagination. For Jason, these orbs, tied to the surrounding tree trunks were architectural objects of outstanding beauty.

After a little investigation, Jason found that importing these spheres for manufacture into the UK wouldn't prove feasible as the cost and logistics were too prohibitive. But the idea of a spherical tree-house suspended from the branches wouldn't leave him and so, in collaboration with a circle of friends with skill sets spanning engineering to airship design, he set about creating the 'tree tent'. Now, when this cleverly engineered and designed structure of canvas, aluminium and wood is suspended by ropes rigged into the trees, a totally new space is created – a liberating one without a footprint, which blends effortlessly into the environment.

Looking at a form like the tree tent in isolation it's difficult to visualise it as fitting comfortably into the landscape, but when sited in a woodland location it looks so natural, as though it's meant to be there.

The Plan

For Jason, this project, like all those he undertakes, had to engage him personally. With his strong belief that woodland and forests are 'places of calm ... relaxing, healing places and somewhere that feels right to be', he dreamed of creating and running his own campsite in a sustainable way as a personally fulfilling business venture.

Jason's big idea was to create an eco woodland hotel out of his tree tents to encourage people to connect with the trees, while his vision and ultimate long-term goal is for his team to 'start travelling the world, fitting tree tents into every forest'.

"Without sounding too much like a tree-hugging hippy, the tree talks to you when you're in a tree tent."

JASON THAWLEY — DESIGNER

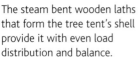

The steam bent wooden laths that form the tree tent's shell provide it with even load distribution and balance.

Design

Approaching this project in the same way he would design any consumer product, Jason's ideas started out as a rough sketch on a piece of paper. He showed it to his friends, each of whom contributed a different approach and knowledge base to the discussion, and modified sketches passed backwards and forwards between them. They wanted to design a structure that was really light but very strong while retaining the feel of a real tent. From there, the original design was drawn up in a 3-D format on the computer and was strength tested using high-spec engineering software. Finally, separate drawings were made and the first prototype developed.

The symmetrical, spherical shape of the Tree Tent encompasses the aesthetics and practicality of this project. A sphere has a central hinging point, which works well for rigging in the trees; it can be tethered easily and the rain runs off it well. It also has important benefits for manufacturing costs – the same parts can be re-used in multiple places, while the number of different specifications is reduced, making reordering easier.

Materials and techniques

A unique space, the tree tent uses an unusual blend of innovative high-end engineering techniques and age-old woodworking skills. The frame is made from the wood of a green ash tree; the sub-frame is aluminium; the ceiling and floor are constructed of plywood, and everything is wrapped in a canvas cover. Lighter than their Canadian alternatives, the tree tents are cheaper to produce, and use fewer, more eco-friendly materials.

The success of the tree tent is down to the collaboration between members of Jason's team, each of whom brought his own specialist talents to the project: Dylan, a woodsman, was experienced in steam bending, an age-old way of steaming wood for 20 minutes in a sealed box and then bending it around a form into the desired shape; while Duncan was a skilled production and automotive engineer; and Alasdair an aircraft engineer. And, as Jason says: 'If there was something we didn't know how to do, we learnt how to do it.'

Interior and styling

Light streams into the tree tent from the circular skylight, while the doorway and window canvas flaps can be rolled down and secured shut.

The tree tent is a unique space – as well as being a practical outdoors environment, it is also a sophisticated piece of high-end design and technology. As a result, there are elements of Jason's interior that echo that time-honoured feel of camping in the wilderness – the 100 per cent heavy-duty cotton canvas, the standard tent maker's material, plus chunky zips and wooden fashioned pegs for securing the window flaps. However, apart from these concessions to tradition, this is a truly modern, forward-looking space with its own sense of adventure and an inspiring separateness.

Jason envisioned the interior having a solid feel, imbued with a utilitarianism but still feeling plush. Above all, there were practical concerns to consider as it needed to be hardwearing, warm and stand up to the elements as well as making the most of the available space. Being a sphere, the space underneath the floor is utilised for storage, while the bed space, with its natural mattresses, extends to the width of the sphere in the area in which you can't stand up. Apart from this cosy bed area, the focal point is the tiny wood burning stove, a dream feature in any semi-permanent tent, and the logs are stored neatly beneath it.

A warm bed and a cosy tent – what else could one need or desire? This unique space has all the romance and comforts of more luxurious and conventional canvas structures but also just happens to be suspended in the air in the magical environment of the woods.

Since first building the tree tent, a bridge and deck area have been added along with a lining for insulation and decorative purposes.

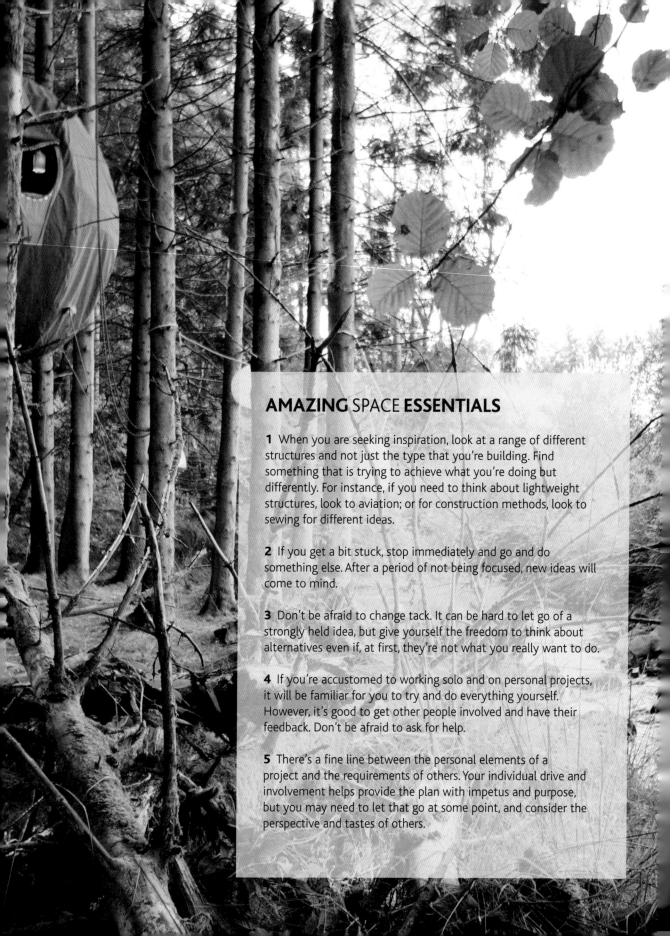

AMAZING SPACE ESSENTIALS

1 When you are seeking inspiration, look at a range of different structures and not just the type that you're building. Find something that is trying to achieve what you're doing but differently. For instance, if you need to think about lightweight structures, look to aviation; or for construction methods, look to sewing for different ideas.

2 If you get a bit stuck, stop immediately and go and do something else. After a period of not being focused, new ideas will come to mind.

3 Don't be afraid to change tack. It can be hard to let go of a strongly held idea, but give yourself the freedom to think about alternatives even if, at first, they're not what you really want to do.

4 If you're accustomed to working solo and on personal projects, it will be familiar for you to try and do everything yourself. However, it's good to get other people involved and have their feedback. Don't be afraid to ask for help.

5 There's a fine line between the personal elements of a project and the requirements of others. Your individual drive and involvement helps provide the plan with impetus and purpose, but you may need to let that go at some point, and consider the perspective and tastes of others.

MIXING
MATERIALS

1 Mixing different materials and forms of manufacture creates a striking contrast. Here the smooth rounded forms of the plastic chairs, lamp and hanging acrylic chair sit alongside the natural elements of the simple wooden table, twig arrangement and textural wool rug.

2 A floating metal frame filled with small wooden bricks is used in this space as a very effective means of partitioning the table area from the rest of the room. Notice how the wood and steel theme is continued in the design of the steel legs of the table and wooden chairs.

3 The smooth, straight lines of the heavy concrete walls and floor set against the soft, textured orange padded chair and rug demonstrate how effective a simple mixing of materials and colours can be.

THE MODULAR PODS

There is something courageous about deciding to build a simple modern building in a traditional rural landscape – there's nowhere to hide, no streetscape or mix of buildings to distract the attention. But that's exactly what farmers George and Julie did; their simple, modern modular building sits alone, with pride, on the brow of a hill, surrounded by sheep and with a view so wide and awe-inspiring that you can literally see the weather coming in off the distant horizon.

Farming is a hard way of life and today's farmers have to diversify and find additional revenue streams to make the land work. George and Julie's vision of building an innovative eco holiday home isn't unique but the path they chose was. Instead of taking the safe option and buying a ready-made structure, they took an enormous risk with an untested designer and an untested product.

ALTHOUGH ALL SMALL-SPACE BUILDS REQUIRE A CERTAIN AMOUNT OF INNOVATION, THERE ARE SOME PEOPLE OUT THERE WHO ARE PREPARED TO PUSH THE BOUNDARIES OF WHAT'S POSSIBLE TO WHOLE NEW LEVELS.

The Plan

George and Julie's family farm was losing money – the couple had to sell some land to repay the bank – and they had long been talking about how best to diversify to make the farm work. Paying off their debts focused George and Julie's minds, and from struggling to come up with a solution, they started to think creatively about how to generate revenue from the amazing natural assets they had in the landscape they owned. Their initial idea was a glamping enterprise and, given that services, drainage and utilities all needed to be considered, they approached architect Sam Booth about building a toilet block on the farm. Approaching it from an alternative perspective, he pointed out that there was little cost difference between their proposal and creating a more substantial structure – a real building, using eco principles, that would function as a self-contained, modular-built eco holiday home. There would be no roughing it or making do; in Sam's book, you don't have to sacrifice comfort for principles.

Sam had long harboured an idea about modular builds and the timing worked for him as well as Julie and George, who instinctively felt that he was a person who shared their ideals and would be easy to work with – an important consideration in any building and design project. Moreover, he suggested that, as he was starting from scratch and this project would, hopefully, be one of many, he wouldn't charge for any design work if he could keep the designs and reuse them. Sam had had a vision, and he wanted something that he could reproduce.

What makes George and Julie's modular construction particularly brave is that it was built as a prototype. Traditionally these are models where the structure has never been attempted before and which are built to test a concept or process, to find out what works and what doesn't. In their case, this first attempt would be the only one – there was no leeway. The prototype had to be right and it had to work first time round.

Design and structure

The modular pods consist of four separate 3m (9ft) square units, which are interlinked and sited on the brow of a hill looking due south. This modular style of design means that any number of units can be fastened together to configure a space in any way you wish. Julie and George chose to connect theirs in a square formation, divided with internal walls. Rather than create totally separate internal spaces, the kitchen and living pods were knocked through into one single space. There is also a spacious master bedroom and a small cleverly designed bathroom. There are separate areas for cooking, washing, sleeping and relaxing, with floor-to-ceiling windows looking out at the ridiculously beautiful view.

The exact size of the building was dictated not by a grandiose design scheme but for pragmatic reasons relating to a series of restrictions. For planning consent, the modular pods had to meet certain technical criteria as to their size and portability. Moving the pieces also meant that there was a limit to the width that was suitable for road transportation, while plywood – the main structural component – is available only in specified sheet sizes.

All these factors dictated the specific height, depth and width of each pod. As is so often the case when looking for an answer to design issues, the correct solution is a straightforward, realistic response to the problems involved.

This build is based on a concept of regular sized, single prefabricated modular units, that form the 'building blocks' of a fully customisable space. They are easily joined together and can be moved and assembled in various numbers and configurations.

Exterior

The exterior of each pod is clad with wooden panels, made from larch and laid in a grid-like structure, which was inspired by the design of wooden palettes. Prefabricated and clipped on to the exterior, their alternate vertical and horizontal placing adds a distinctive linear pattern, each panel reflecting the light differently, depending on the time of day and weather conditions.

As the pods are off-grid, power is provided via two large solar panels, which are linked to a battery, while the cooker and shower are heated by bottled gas.

A decking area beyond the glass doors at the end of the building, cleverly opening up and using the space beyond the modular pods' footprint.

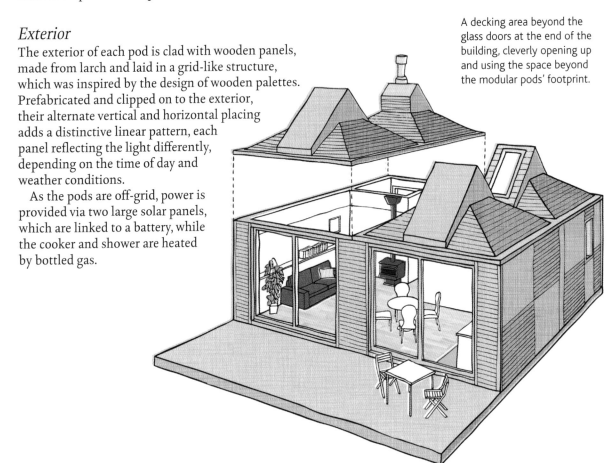

Interior and styling

Some small-space solutions are preferable to just folding or hiding things away. In the pod, the kitchen has been built as a piece of furniture, raised off the ground and making the interior feel more spacious. Similarly, no pipes and cabling are visible throughout, while the wiring was thought out at the design stage; it is built in and concealed within the walls. In a similar vein, the interior horizontal shelf that runs around the walls is not only part of the structure of the building but also functions as a decorative feature.

Julie has a good eye and her taste is simple, modern and graphic in style. Working alongside Sam's wife Maggie, an artist, the mod pods' colour palette began to take shape. Maggie's brainwave was to paint just a small area on each interior wall, believing that this approach would have more impact than painting the wall in its entirety. They found that on a windowless wall, a patch with colour creates a focal point, providing interest and helping the eye to linger there. The overall effect was to make the space feel more restful and calming, especially if the panel of colour was placed at eye level.

This is no dingy holiday home – lightness and brightness abound. The vast glass doors that face south open up onto the landscape and help the building seem bigger. This space is warm, comfortable and environmentally friendly as well as simple and elegant – proof that small can be beautiful.

Three square skylights open up to provide additional ventilation and act as light wells, dispersing light across the conical ceiling into the pod. The building is located in a certified 'dark skies' area and the position and design of the skylights means that you can enjoy stargazing whether lying in bed or sitting on the sofa.

Clutter is shut away in cupboards, leaving out only a few carefully chosen things to create interesting still lives.

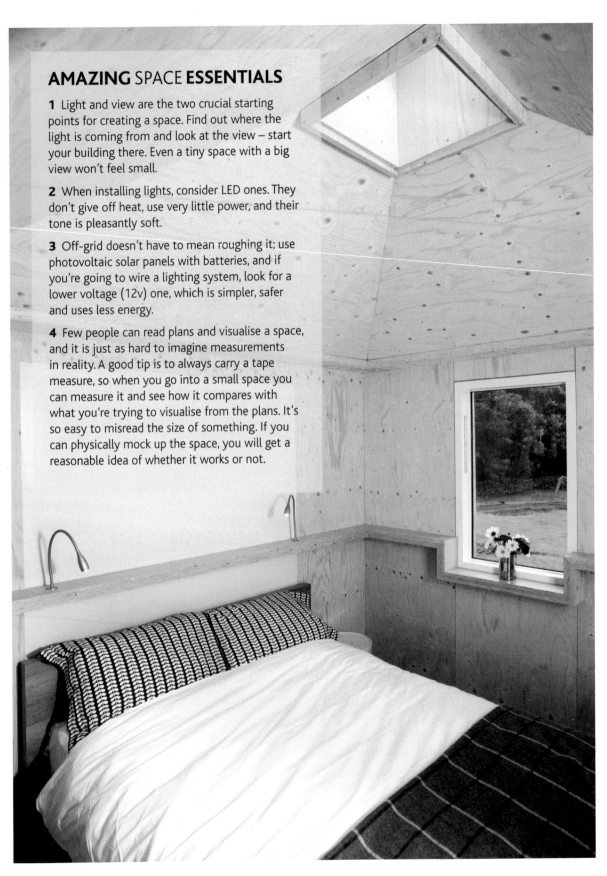

AMAZING SPACE ESSENTIALS

1 Light and view are the two crucial starting points for creating a space. Find out where the light is coming from and look at the view – start your building there. Even a tiny space with a big view won't feel small.

2 When installing lights, consider LED ones. They don't give off heat, use very little power, and their tone is pleasantly soft.

3 Off-grid doesn't have to mean roughing it; use photovoltaic solar panels with batteries, and if you're going to wire a lighting system, look for a lower voltage (12v) one, which is simpler, safer and uses less energy.

4 Few people can read plans and visualise a space, and it is just as hard to imagine measurements in reality. A good tip is to always carry a tape measure, so when you go into a small space you can measure it and see how it compares with what you're trying to visualise from the plans. It's so easy to misread the size of something. If you can physically mock up the space, you will get a reasonable idea of whether it works or not.

1 This new kitchen in an older building retains the original structural beams – lending the space an appealing honesty.

2 This kitchen successfully conveys a simple modern eco look, where the materials themselves – as opposed to added decorative items – do the talking.

GET THE LOOK

MODERN
ECO

3 The different tones that are visible when building with recycled wood are celebrated in this space, rather than disguised.

4 Although there is a lot of wood here, clean straight, lines and geometric shapes give this room structure, while the floating shelves, table and open staircase provide a much-needed sense of lightness.

RECYCLED SPACES

Avoiding waste and saving money while doing your bit for the environment is no bad thing, and creating something that is high style while re-using materials has great appeal. This chapter is full of finding ways to give new life to materials and objects, something which brings its own joy. Sourcing the items too can be fun, and although some materials definitely need to be new for safety considerations, there are legitimate reasons for looking at how materials can be reused and items intended for other uses that can be re-purposed to create something new and interesting.

BEFORE...

THE
Majestic
BUS

Rob and Layla Robinson dreamt of creating a desirable holiday home on the site of their smallholding, nestled on the side of a picturesque valley in the Welsh border. But turning the dilapidated 1960s bus that sat in their barn into this would prove to be a challenge not for the faint-hearted.

With its panels removed, no back window and an interior full of junk, the bus that sat in Rob and Layla's barn had definitely seen better days. But for Rob there was 'nothing quite like it – beautiful, private, tranquil and relaxing, the bus and the spectacular landscape seemed to fit together'. Viewed from the outside, such vision takes an enormous leap of faith, but sometimes we can't achieve things in life without exactly that.

WHEN I TALK ABOUT SMALL SCALE BUILDERS NEEDING BIG IMAGINATIONS, ROB SPRINGS TO MIND. HIS COMMITMENT AND CREATIVY HAS HELPED CREATE THE MOST INCREDIBLE OF SPACES.

The Plan

When Rob and Layla purchased the bus it was already partially dismantled, and their original intention was to convert it into a campervan. However, after owning it for two years, the impracticality of their plan became patently clear: the bus was just too big and unwieldy to become a 'go anywhere' campervan. Rob had seen buses converted into holiday or temporary accommodation and his mind was open to the possibilities. For him, the bus, with its curved lined coachwork, chunky chrome fittings, classic signwriting and paintwork, big windows and numerous skylights, possessed the beauty that is characteristic of many 1950s and 1960s commercial vehicles – all lovely aesthetic features that soon became obsolete.

Throughout the project, Rob and Layla were guided by their eco principles and shared lifelong interest in 'doing the greenest thing possible'. Living off-grid, without access to the national grid, made them acutely aware of what power they were using and why. The bus project needed to follow suit and would provide a unique opportunity for their guests to dip their toes into an off-grid lifestyle.

Exterior

The decisions regarding the exterior of the bus were very straightforward: to repair and replace the rusty and missing panels, refit or replace the trims, and restore the paintwork and chrome to their original glory. Some structural restoration work had already been done, but that work needed to be completed and the bus reassembled before the real work could begin on the interior.

An outside decked area completes the bus's transformation, extending the space and connecting it to the surrounding landscape.

Interior

Once the seats were removed (and recycled), Rob and Layla started planning the interior. They drew the layout onto the floor in chalk, re-sizing and re-positioning as necessary and chipping away at the different possibilities until the project developed its own flow. At this point the plan was transposed onto paper.

They decided to create two main areas: one for eating and cooking, the other for seating and sleeping, with bathroom facilities provided separately in a nearby section of the barn. One of the key layout decisions was the positioning of the dining table in the cab area. Rob had initially wanted to keep the cab area as it was to retain the original character of the bus, but moving the table to the front put it close to the kitchen area and made the whole space more flexible. Communality, comfort and multi-functionalism were all factored into the design, with the addition of a wood burning stove, king-size bed, along with a vintage chair and L-shaped sofa providing a big U-shaped seating area in a comfortable configuration.

Choice of materials and fixtures

Bearing in mind the rural nature of the project and Rob and Layla's eco principles, recycled wood was the only option when it came to choosing the primary material for the bus's interior.

By sorting through their local sawmill's bulk orders of firewood bundles (a motley collection of imperfect oak and wood of differing thicknesses and sizes), Rob was able to collect enough large pieces to build the work surfaces, shelves and other features. Additional pinewood was supplied by a gardening client who was dismantling and ripping out an old sauna and wanted to dispose of it.

As vintage caravan fans, Rob and Layla were able to drawn on some familiar and well-loved caravan space-saving concepts. For instance, the L-shaped seating area pulls out to become another double bed, utilising the back and seat cushions as a mattress. Under-bed and seating storage, another caravan favourite, takes the form of vintage wooden fruit crates picked up in the local market.

The original bus fittings – the steering wheel, speedometer, door handles, dashboard and signage all possessed great character and, when cleaned up and polished, earned their place in the remodelled interior.

Rob and Layla weren't seeking the perfection and smooth finish of high-grade wood, preferring a rougher, more textural finish. The fittings – such as the taps, light fittings and door handles – were also all repurposed. The shelves, suspended by rough jute ropes, contribute to this look of simple rustic beauty, while the two-ringed gas cooker (which runs on propane gas) which was salvaged from an old caravan belonging to Layla's grandmother, helps carry the vintage style of the bus's exterior through to the interior.

The project used recycled materials whenever it was cost-effective to do so. The pair also tried to source items locally, wherever possible. That's not to say that more of them couldn't have been reclaimed but they had to work within budget and sometimes buying new and making it look nice was a more achievable option.

AMAZING SPACE ESSENTIALS

1 It's daunting to think of everything at once, so concentrate on just one thing at a time.

2 Don't get bogged down in every single detail. Rob and Layla spent a lot of time worrying about how the big exterior panels would go back, especially refitting the extensive back windscreen – would it go back at all? It literally needed hitting with large pieces of wood – a heart-stopping moment.

3 Try to shut your brain down at times or you'll be overwhelmed. It often didn't feel as though the project was going to work at all until it was almost finished. It was only then that Andy and Layla were able to relax when it was finally decorated and they could admire their creation.

3

4

RECYCLED
WOOD

1 These worn wooden crates have been repurposed as simple desk legs, providing support as well as additional storage.

2 Using old doors as collage material, this staircase wall has the appearance of being haphazard but in truth is well thought out and executed. Each door is held within a shallow frame and has a simple latch fixing. The doors are cut to fit and the entire frame floats off the staircase in a precise fashion.

3 Piet Hein Eek is a renowned Dutch artist who designs and creates furniture using recycled scrap wood, such as this decorative dining table and sideboard. With their high quality finish, these are extremely sophisticated pieces of furniture, despite the fundamental nature of the source material.

4 Weathered pieces of bleached driftwood are used simply in this bedroom, giving the space character and tone to balance the white bed linen, painted floorboards and unfinished plaster walls.

THE *eco* HUT

IF SOMEONE WAS TO ASK ME FOR MY VISION OF A PERFECT FORESTER'S HUT IN THE WOODS I'D PROBABLY DRAW THIS ONE. WHILE IT MAY BE PHYSICALLY SMALL, THE LEVEL OF AMBITION BEHIND THIS PROJECT IS MASSIVE.

To design and build something from scratch is a big achievement for anybody. To do so using recycled and ethically sourced materials, while keeping the project totally in keeping with the natural environment, is a massive one. For Tim Sands, the young designer and owner of this woodland cabin, it's even more remarkable given that this is the first building he has designed and that the project necessitated him developing carpentry skills that he didn't previously have.

The cabin is a simple, rough and ready wooden structure, sited in its own plot of woodland on top of a hill overlooking Lake Windermere and the surrounding fells. The majestic distant views change with the seasons and are particularly spectacular in winter, when the trees are bare and snow is visible on the surrounding hillsides. Although The Eco Hut functions primarily as a shelter, the main focus of this building (and the real magic of this project) isn't the hut itself but the great outdoors.

The Plan

For Tim, owning his own plot of land and building a hut on it had been a dream since childhood. Generations of his family had lived in this area and he grew up here, loving the outdoor life. A design and technology teacher for whom learning (particularly practical skills) has always been a joy, it was therefore a natural progression for him to go from purchasing a piece of woodland to learning about it and, ultimately, to tending its trees. This necessitated working with tools and equipment that had to be transported up and down the hill – heavy work. Tim frequently got cold and wet doing it, so he decided that what he needed was a hut; somewhere to store his tools and felled wood and a place to which he could retreat to dry off and warm up.

A ready-made structure purchased from a superstore or garden centre was never going to be Tim's style. He had a rough idea of what he wanted his hut to look like and knew that the exterior should resemble a traditional cabin. When he was given a book about quirky, unusual sheds, ideas soon started to form and he was inspired by several of the sheds he saw. Having no clue as to what size the building should be, he started to plot things out ... literally. Using a space at school, he started figuring out the size and basic plan of the hut. By pacing it out and using a metal tape measure and some chairs as the corner markers, the project took shape.

Exterior

The steepness of the hillside and Tim's desire for the building not to have a big footprint on the landscape dictated that the hut would be best built on a level platform, flush with the hillside at the back and with six wide steps at the front. Essentially, it is a simple, sturdy structure, constructed entirely in wood, with a traditional look. The roof is made of cedar shingles while the walls are clad in wavy-edged larch panels. The windows look out over the front to Windermere and to woodland on one side.

Tim didn't create foundations as it would have meant putting concrete into the woodland. Instead, he used eight treated posts and dug a series of two-foot holes, lined the bases with stone, then dropped in the posts and replaced the soil and rocks, compacting each layer. Old school hard work!

Twenty years or so ago, the trees growing in this forest had a commercial value and were cut, as evidenced by the hillside tracks, deeply worn by the lumber vehicles. Now the forest needs to be regularly maintained, a job that led to Tim's need for a shelter.

AMAZING SPACE ESSENTIALS

1 Don't get started on your project without doing your homework thoroughly first: read, research and learn up!

2 Don't be afraid to ask for help. People will love to hear about what you are doing, and many will have ideas or opinions that could prove useful. Everyone loves a two-way conversation, so ask for help or advice and it will be given.

3 Write down your plans and ideas, draw them or make a list. Having something on paper makes it easier to explain your vision to other people, helping them to understand and get involved – not everyone can visualise.

4 Rethink, reuse and recycle instead of buying everything new from a big store. Refuse to pay top dollar and support the small local guy. He has the product, the knowledge and the guidance.

5 And always remember when working with wood – measure twice ... cut once!

Materials and techniques

The hut uses locally felled wood wherever possible, with the wood taken to a local sawmill and cut into the required sizes. The larch wood for the hut's panels came from a friend's land in Wales where the tree trunks are pulled clear by shire horses, a traditional method that minimises the need for wide tracks to be cut through the forest. The logs are pulled out lengthways, so the only damage to the ground is the trail left by the horses' hooves. Apart from this, as many of the other materials as possible were sourced within a few miles of the project.

Tim's primary skills involve working on cars, metalwork and 3-D design, so his experience of woodwork and construction was extremely limited. However, he relishes a challenge and the opportunity to learn and develop new skills. By studying woodworking books and watching videos on the internet, he learnt how best to construct his dream hut on the hill. Piece by piece and driven by necessity, he figured out a plan and decided to 'wing it'.

His friends helped, too. Friends from his childhood and school, plus their friends, all chipped in, and their shared experiences on the project cemented their friendship and camaraderie. At the end of a day's work, they would cook burgers over a fire and share a beer. Everyone was willing to participate and enjoyed taking part – they learnt together as well as sharing the mistakes.

"If you have an idea, seize it. Ask people's advice. Be graceful, listen intently and ask questions. Then once you have learnt a new skill, teach others."

TIM SANDS – OWNER

Interior and styling

Tim made a list of the essentials he felt he needed inside the hut: storage, a wood burner, a workbench, a sink and somewhere to sit. Everything else could be fitted in around these. As many of the items as possible were found, rescued or donated, with objects only purchased new where absolutely necessary. Once these items had been sourced, Tim planned the layout accordingly, their position dictated by the nature of what he had been able to acquire. Tim discovered that everything made its own space, and thus the subsequent interior plan took shape.

During the build Tim had to learn a number of new skills, roof laying among them. Occasionally mistakes were made (such as the time when he measured the wood frames for his windows incorrectly) but for Tim this was all part of the journey.

Tim carried his recycling principles through to the hut's interior, collecting all the necessary items in magpie fashion. The door, including locks and hinge, was purchased at a car boot sale, the stainless-steel sink came from a skip, the windows were donated, and the wall cupboards were in the process of being thrown out at his school before they were saved by Tim. The second-hand wood burning stove takes pride of place in the centre of the space.

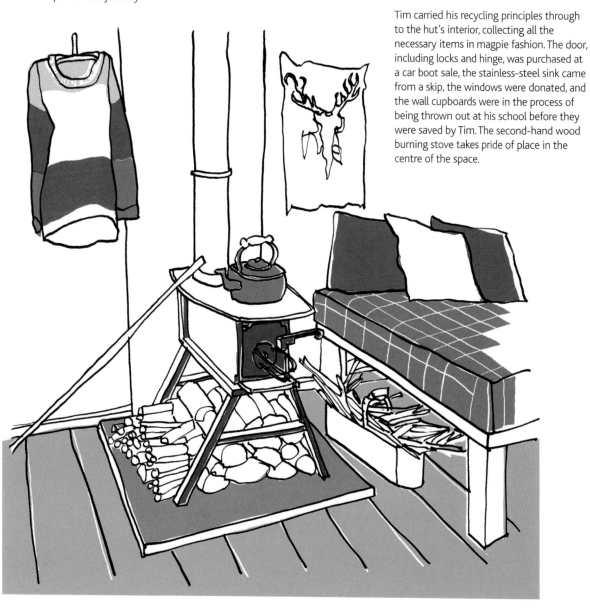

Aside from The Eco Hut, Tim's ongoing project is a visual online blog, which acts as a scrapbook. He collects images of everything he likes and posts them on the site. All of his interests get a look in, including sheds, cars, girls, architecture and design – the whole gamut.

As this was the natural collection point for his imagination, it proved to be a ready-made moodboard for how he wanted the interior of the hut to look. Tim set about creating an interior that had genuine charm, an earthiness and honesty that included paintings, sketches and textile artworks by his girlfriend Julie as well as natural hand-woven textiles, enamel and tin. Earnest and simple materials in keeping with this honest, but beautiful build.

NOTE
Tim's hut was completed in the summer of 2012, but later that year it was set alight by arsonists. After a period of contemplation, Tim has decided to rebuild it. Offers of help and support have been overwhelming.

CABIN
STYLE

1 Here the regular width horizontal wall planking and natural coloured floor lend this room a typical cabin look, while the modern chair provides an unexpected, fresh counterpoint to the gentle, natural tones.

2 The simple architectural shape and horizontal wooden boards give this super stylish urban sewing shed a touch of classic cabin style.

3 Clad with highly textured and distinctively shaped sawn logs, the wall of this living room acts as a dramatic anchor and a focal point. The Yves Klein blue painted wooden stag's head and comfortable upholstered furniture with rounded forms make this a quirky, modern interpretation of cabin style.

4 This blue painted interior of a musician's modern log cabin is a simple space. No attempt has been made to make the interior 'woody' but in keeping it relatively simple and undemanding your eye is immediately drawn to the real thing outside the window.

THE

CIRCUS

THEATRE

Using a caravan as a starting point, young actor Michael Imerson and his troupe dreamt of converting an ordinary nondescript vehicle into something quite unique. They wanted to create a fantastical touring caravan, which opens up to become a performance space, with its own scenery and mini-museum.

Their caravan theatre was to be a modern version of the showmen's caravans that you might have seen in Wild West or in travelling circus shows – but this one would use Science-Fiction, Victorian and futuristic elements in its styling.

MOST OF THE BUILD'S THAT FEATURE WITHIN THIS BOOK CONCENTRATE ON PRACTICAL, SIMPLE WAYS TO FIND SOLUTIONS TO EVERYDAY SMALL SPACE PROBLEMS. THIS ONE DOES JUST THAT, BUT WITH A FANTASTICAL ELEMENT THAT LIFTS IT WAY BEYOND THE EVERYDAY.

The Plan

With a background in street theatre and circus, Michael was keen to find a unique and theatrical way of making his shows as distinctive as possible while enhancing his creative performance. As with many of the projects featured in this book, the inspiration for this space did not come from nowhere – along with his co-performers, he formerly had a tiny set that was fixed to the back of a tricycle, which was easily mobile and self-contained. He noticed how his audience responded well to his idiosyncratic performance vehicle and the way it intrigued and engaged them.

From this initial tricycle concept, Michael worked up the idea for a fully mobile, recycled caravan – a visually dense performance vehicle, which would act as an installation, which would continue to generate interest even when it was closed up. Built specifically as the stage and backdrop to a spectacular show about travelling through the imagination, the style of the caravan conversion would have to be nothing short of fantastic in its functionality and design. The decision was made to work up the caravan within a Steampunk style – a retro/futuristic sub-genre that mixes different historical, sci-fi, industrial and material elements to create a fantasy world.

The Circus Theatre gradually opens to reveal the museum within. When operating as a theatre, the curtain is closed and the performance is conducted in front of the curtains hiding the caravan's contents and increasing the sense of wonder and mystery.

Design and structure

Michael tracked down a caravan that was both in the style he was after and appeared structurally sound, and set about the business of converting it carefully and safely in order to retain the vehicle's structural integrity. Many of the original caravan's interior fittings and appliances were removed and recycled, while other elements which suited the ultimate design style, such as the nautical windows, were retained. In order to open up what was originally an enclosed internal space, one side of the caravan was removed and replaced with two large plywood doors opening outwards on hinges, thereby effectively turning the vehicle into a stage and the interior of the caravan into what was to become a fantastical Steampunk themed mini-museum.

Style and finishing touches

Decorative elements of paintings, old machinery, broken clocks and picture books were all added to create the inventive mechanical fantasy effect that Michael and his fellow performers were after. The idea was to use familiar styles, such as Victoriana, as well as key features of literature, history and art in such a way that people could relate to the individual cultural elements while experiencing a new, jumbled-up version of the familiar. The appeal of this sort of style lies in its dream-like quality where the audience's imagination is challenged and encouraged – it's an easy journey to another world.

The entire caravan is painted in a decorative style using maritime and Steampunk imagery, so that even when the caravan is closed the style and theatrical element is self-evident. When the doors are opened the background to the stage is a large red velvet curtain, which at the end of the show is drawn back to reveal the fantasical museum within the caravan itself.

The small storage cupboards high on the walls have been retained, have been lit by fairy lights and contain the intriguing museum displays within them. The original bathroom area has been stripped out, replaced by a glass dome on a pedestal containing a decorative still life.

Now finished, Michael plans to travel around the United Kingdom, towing his super-stylised caravan to different music and arts festivals. Using it as a unique performance space, putting on a show in a memorable way and transporting the audience into a world beyond the actual performance itself.

AMAZING SPACE ESSENTIALS

1 Theme your space. Finding a theme for your space can be a great way of imbuing it with character and style, provided that it is something that represents you in a genuine way rather than an idea taken totally out of context.

2 Do your research. In this project Michael based his Steampunk design theme on the specific show that the caravan has been designed for. But generally, all stylistic themes come from somewhere – they have a history and take inspiration from looking back to a previous point in time. For example, Steampunk references Victoriana and the Industrial Revolution. Research your theme by looking back at its influences and you will find a rich source of inspiration and ideas.

3 Open your mind to ideas. Films, books and magazines can help you find that spark of inspiration, and also museums, interesting shops and galleries. A snippet of an overheard conversation can start you off, what someone is wearing, or just a random thought – it is about being open to an idea and then developing it and making it your own.

WE ALL DREAM ABOUT HAVING SOMEWHERE WE CAN GO TO ESCAPE THE HUSTLE AND BUSTLE OF EVERYDAY LIFE. SO WHAT ABOUT THIS LITTLE PIECE OF PARADISE BY THE WATER'S EDGE?

THE FISHING SHACK

This fishing shack on the lake is one man's dream, albeit one that many of us share. Rob Cowan, the owner and designer, wanted the shack to have integrity, and he looked towards the frontier shacks and huts of the American Midwest for inspiration. It proved a rich source of ideas for natural materials, proportions, design and aesthetics – indeed Rob was so inspired by Midwestern designs that he decided to use their traditional construction methods of mortise and tenon joints, working with locally-sourced wavy-edged Douglas fir wood.

A move away from this tradition has been the large floor-to-ceiling window overlooking the lake. It fills the shack's interior with light, and who wouldn't want to sit on the cosy sofa by a roaring fire and enjoy that amazing view over the tranquil water? With its picturesque location on the lake's edge, simple wooden construction, big deck and overhanging cedar-shingled roof this is a warm and comfortable shelter, which is engaged with its surrounding spectacular landscape.

THE Cob House

THIS HOUSE IS JUST INCREDIBLE – IT'S GENIUS. I LOVE THE WAY IT HAS BEEN BUILT FROM MATERIALS THAT HAVE BEEN SOURCED FROM THE SURROUNDING LANDSCAPE, AND THE BUILDING TECHNIQUES USED ARE TRADITIONAL AND SIMPLE – NOT A SINGLE POWER TOOL WAS USED IN IT'S CONSTRUCTION AND THE COST TO BUILD WAS VIRTUALLY NOTHING.

Most of us nowadays have no option but to build our homes out of anything other than conventional materials such as brick, cement, wood, stone or concrete. However, it was only after industrialisation and the advent of cheaper transportation in the early nineteenth century that building materials and bricks could be more easily manufactured and delivered all over the country and became as widely used as they are today.

Even today, about one-third of the world's population still lives in houses made of centuries-old earthen construction materials. The idea certainly isn't a new one. What makes this project so surprising was the startling economy of this project – its creator, Michael Buck managed to complete the build for a total spend equivalent to a meal out for four in a fancy restaurant!

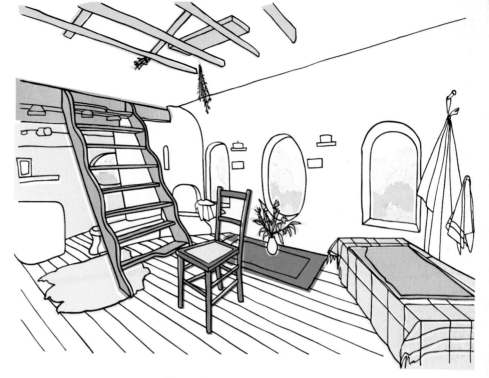

It is simply furnished, the building materials and construction methods are on show, there is integrity to both the interior and exterior appearance. Gentle curves, deep reveals and curved windows and doors create a magical and comfortable atmosphere.

The Plan

This whole project was kept as simple in possible in both approach and construction. There were no fancy blueprints drawn up – the planning and drawing out of ideas was all sketched up, quite unbelievably, on one side of a used envelope.

The key material used for construction was to be 'cob' – a loose term for a composite material made of a mix of earth and other natural elements. Historically, the materials that went into making cob buildings varied depending on location. In the United Kingdom, for example, these houses were usually made by mixing a clay sub-soil with sand, soil, straw and water, and these were then trampled or mixed together by people or animals – more modern methods use a tractor and the addition of gravel-type materials. The worked-up material would be laid in courses on top of a stone foundation, allowing each level to dry out, shrink and harden before adding the next.

A key feature of this type of building is that the materials can be locally sourced. Michael Buck, the creator of the Cob House, wanted to see if he could live a sustainable life, which included building a house using only natural materials from the communal farmland on which he was working. Such was his dedication to the project that he went to the extremes of growing the straw for the thatched roof in advance, sourcing the cob from the local land, and involving his friends in 'pottling' it into place.

Exterior

Cob walls are built thickly and provide a natural insulation, which Michael boosted further by adding sheep's wool to the roof area. Along with the thatched roof, they work to keep the house both warm in winter and cool in the summer.

Most of the outer walls are plastered using cow dung, which is naturally a fibrous product. 'Marigold', 'Crystal' and 'Mist' were the three obliging cows, and Michael has kindly acknowledged their contribution by writing their names in a line in the plaster along with the other folk who also worked on this project.

Interior

Because certain design features of the building are included in the structure itself, the shelves, alcoves, doors and windows are all formed within the actual shaping of the space, and this enabled Michael to build his furniture into the shape as he went along. With this type of construction, tackling the building as a whole entity, it takes on a certain aesthetic: a rounded handmade-looking sculptural form.

The interior space is simple, with just one open plan room, that contains a small kitchen area, table and chairs, a wood burning stove and a sleeping platform accessed by a small 'paddle' ladder which Michael found sawn in two on a rubbish skip. Michael's environmentally friendly principles follow

The pitch of the thatched roof was important as, coupled with a deep overhang, it enables the rain to drip off from one piece of straw to the next and negates the need for guttering.

the water supply, which is natural spring water. Channelled from several small existing streams through a clay pipe it forms a small spout from which all the fresh water from the house is collected. His fridge is natural too – a shaded water-filled well in the woods which keeps items cool whatever the weather.

Tapping into a growing trend within the eco and sustainable movement to look again at the use of clay, mud, and straw as building materials, the Cob House is a stunning, and exceptional realisation of ancient building techniques and thrifty values. It is extraordinary how little this build cost, and along its charm and character, Michael's building is, in its way, a wake up call to a world where housing is so expensive and building costs high.

1

2

1 Fairytale design creates a magical, other-worldly feeling by conjuring up an atmosphere of woodland whimsy. Here apart from the large windows that almost place you in the trees beyond, the deerskin rug, the throw over the back of the sofa complete with antlered stag, and the tiny woodland creatures on the window ledge all help set the scene for some fireside tales.

2 This tiny side table acts as its own fairytale still-life world. The tall, delicate twigs have a group of fake feathered birds perched on them and add height and majesty to this arrangement, while the books and precious looking glass dome on the table surface continue the theme.

GET THE LOOK

FAIRYTALE
DESIGN

3 This bathroom has an almost a medieval, castle-like feel. The long net curtains are suspended on a rough branch, while the stone clad bath itself seems to be suspended in the trees themselves.

4 Outside elements brought inside seem can take on a different character. Here the plant is allowed to grow – clinging on to the wall and around the mirror – reminding you that it has a life of its own, while the collection of botanical drawings and specimens on the desk add a human touch.

THE
BEER MOTH

TRANSFORMING OLD ABANDONED VEHICLES LIKE THIS INTO INSPIRATIONAL SPACES TO LIVE AND WORK TAKES CARE, PASSION, AND INGENUITY. THIS BEAST OF A TRUCK IS A UNIQUE EXERCISE IN CREATIVITY AND FREEDOM OF EXPRESSION.

A former military fire truck, this 1956 Commer Q4 has been on quite a journey since Walter Micklethwaite spotted a 'for sale' advertisement for it in a military vehicles classified column. After a four day trip from Kent to the spectacular setting of the Scottish Highlands and a lot of work later, the old truck now benefits from a bespoke canvas cover which, when it's rolled up and the sides are lowered, opens the interior up and connects it to this glorious landscape.

Fitted out with an amalgam of period, vintage and hand-made pieces, it has been transformed into an artful, comfortable and inspired little holiday home for two people. A delightfully macho yet creative repurposed vintage vehicle, this is a campervan like no other.

Professionally made, the new canvas roof with its roll up sides worked out to be the most expensive part of the project.

The Plan

A reclamation junkie, Walter loves collecting interesting bits and pieces, often with no specific end use for the objects in mind. The 'Beer Moth', as this vehicle is now known, is an expression of many of his interests and acquisitions and, as he says, 'an exercise in recycling things that don't necessarily cost much but have a patina, a bit of a story and a bit of age'.

The original seeds for this idea were sown several years previously, while Walter was still living in the city, when he seriously considered creating a mobile bar from an old vintage vehicle. Having moved to the wilds of Scotland to live on some land his parents had purchased over 40 years previously, Walter saw the potential to create a business in this wonderful landscape.

Walter's first thought was to build yurts (portable circular Mongolian tents) on the land, but it wasn't long before he decided that a vehicle would be a better way to give people the opportunity to truly escape for a short break while also getting to stay in a really quirky space. Inspired by the ideas of renowned small

Attached to the side of the vehicle a container box acts as excellent storage for the logs used to fuel the wood burning stove.

Originally Walter put a Rayburn cooker which he salvaged from a derelict cottage in the Beer Moth, however it proved impractical due to its weight and was later replaced by a handmade steel stove.

space visionary Lloyd Kahn, Walter knew what he had to do. For him, the old truck was aesthetically beautiful, and he relished the idea of creating a warm, micro-sized home inside it.

Design

Walter's on-site workshop also serves as a collection point full of various pieces of furniture and items that he has sourced from reclamation yards and skips over the years. Always having a number of projects on the go at any one time, he never knows when a creative spark might be lit and the use for a specific object might emerge.

The interior layout was drawn up to fit in the basic requirements of a bed, cooker table and chairs within this limited space, while also leaving room for access both to the door at the back of the truck and to allow the side of the truck to fold flat when the

canvas is rolled up, which makes a small deck area. To give extra internal headroom, Walter raised the roof height of the truck by a foot.

Materials and styling

Aesthetically, Walter didn't want the style of the truck's interior to be enslaved by any particular historic period but instead wanted to create a more romantic and whimsical feel, which captures the imagination. The truck has a homespun and utilitarian feel, a mixture of the macho seriousness of the truck itself and the homestead cosy interior. That these two somewhat opposing approaches work together is principally due to two factors – the integrity of the material and finishes used, along with The Beer Moth's ability to open up at the sides, allowing the internal and external to merge and become one space.

The Beer Moth interior is a mix of reclaimed and recycled furniture. The 1.2m (4ft) wide Victorian brass bed was sourced from a classified ad in the local paper, for example.

Most of the items in the truck were recycled and many were acquired free of charge. The old oak parquet flooring for example, was rescued from a Tudor manor house, had been sitting around in rubble sacks for over eight years, waiting for a suitable use to arise. Other items were sourced from classified adverts, recycled from old caravans or cottages or in the case of the rear steps (which were formed from an old fire escape), found at the tip.

As Walter says, 'the beauty is in the detail', and he appreciates that it isn't just the large items of furniture that tell the story. Little finishing details play a large part in giving The Beer Moth its charm and character. The kitchen equipment, mugs, plates, washing bowls, tea towels and cushions on the bed all have a simplicity to their design, and a utilitarian, crafts-based, cabin style to them. Simple stripes, plaids, cotton, enamel, wood and wools all work together to make this an interesting and quirky living, but not overly styled space. It has the feeling of items accumulated over time, in an economical and thoughtful way.

The truck's transformation took six months from its original purchase. Now fully fitted out for holiday accommodation, it is compromised by its weight for use as a true road vehicle, but is, nevertheless, still movable.

AMAZING SPACE ESSENTIALS

1 Try to tell a story with your build. For Walter, this was the romance of the open road, and getting away from it all.

2 Look at what you have lying around and think about how those items and materials can be used and recycled in your project.

3 Don't ignore or discard things because they are old and used or show telltale signs of wear – they have a history and add character to a project.

4 Make certain that the space you build is easy to use and not complicated – a space can be whimsical but it should still be practical too.

5 Ensure that your space is fit for purpose. Fit proper insulation, drainage and other essentials as necessary and don't cut corners.

MAKING YOUR
AMAZING SPACE
A REALITY

TAKING THOSE
FIRST STEPS

None of the projects featured within this book could have happened without an initial idea or flash of inspiration, which has then been followed up with a lot of energy, self-belief and determination. But that initial vision needs careful planning and preparation in order to turn it into a physical reality. This is true whether your project is an ambitious new build, a small retro-repair or renovation, or a shed at the bottom of the garden.

With any small-scale project, the temptation is to think that small equals easy. In fact, attention to detail and careful planning are as important here as they are in any major construction project. The importance of having clear designs, setting yourself a realistic budget and drawing up a considered plan of action for your build cannot be overstated. All these things will need to be properly thought through if you are to minimise potential problems and maximise the enjoyment of the physical making of your Amazing Space.

You may feel that these are skills and knowledge that you already have, or partially have. But with a deliverable plan to work to, as well as a clear idea of what it is you want from your space, there is every chance that you will begin embarking on what could be a long and extremely rewarding journey. What follows are a few guidelines, as to how you can go about taking those first practical steps, as well as all the potential pitfalls and tricky questions that you will need to ask yourself along the way.

Having read the 'Thinking up your Amazing Space' section of this book and having seen the variety of projects covered within the other chapters in this book you should have formed a good idea of what it is you want from your own space and which elements you would like to include in it. But it doesn't hurt to get those thoughts on paper! In fact, this is the first (and key) step — as there is something about writing this information down on a piece of paper that focuses the mind and helps you map out the potential strengths and weaknesses of your own idea. Stick it up on your notice board. It will act as a good reminder of your intentions and will keep you on track when things get complicated.

My Project

FIRST ASK YOURSELF...

★ Who will be using the space and what will they be using it for?

★ Do I have any specific design requirements?

★ Do I have a budget?

★ Do I have an idea of when I would like the work started and completed?

★ Do I have the relevant knowledge and skill sets to complete all the aspects of the project myself, or do I need to engage knowledgeable and skilled people who can help me?

GOING IT ALONE OR ENGAGING A *designer* OR *architect?*

Once you've asked yourself those first tricky questions, you'll need to ask yourself the biggest one of all – are you happy to go it alone or do you want to employ a designer or architect to help you along the way?

If you have the confidence and knowledge to design and realise your own Amazing Space plans then this can be an incredibly rewarding experience. However if you are thinking about taking this approach you need to be completely honest with yourself about both your abilities and the time that you will be able to dedicate to the project. To an extent, the level of knowledge required to develop and execute your own plans depends on the type of space you are planning, but often even the simplest of projects needs help along the way from a specialist.

So what are the pros and cons of going it alone versus employing a designer or architect? A designer will, of course, cost money, their fees are usually based on a percentage of the total build value. But they will have already developed draft plans, which are often just sketches, that are usually done 'at risk' – i.e. the designer takes a punt that you will like what they are proposing and decide on them to take the work forward (see fees box p186). But in return you get a huge amount of expertise and support through the design and creative process, which can be more valuable than the fees charged, as this can provide both peace of mind and ease of process, and might actually end up as a quantifiable cash saving too, as they should be able to foresee many of the potential pitfalls and risks that can come up in any project.

A designer or architect will also be able to take whatever ideas you have gathered, be they a simple list of likes and dislikes or more developed thoughts, and interpret and embellish them into a concrete plan.

DESIGNERS AND ARCHITECTS

Designers and architects come in all shapes and sizes; they may be one-man bands who specialise in small domestic work or companies that specialise in small builds or loft conversions, or garden studios, etc. They may be specialists in working with certain types of materials or particular buildings or vehicles, for instance there are reputable and experienced companies that import, design and build retro Airstream caravans. Whichever style of specialist is most appropriate for your project ask yourself the following questions:

★ Do you think the person or company you have chosen is able to do the work?

★ Have you taken up references and are they good?

★ Have you seen examples of their work – and would you be happy with this standard?

★ Do you think you would be able to work with them?

★ Are they able to meet with your timeline?

★ Do they understand your vision clearly and share in what you are trying to achieve?

★ Sales talk is one thing but actually working with someone and dealing with issues and hiccups is another. Before you decide on someone, ask yourself whether you feel confident in expressing yourself in a clear and articulate manner. Is this person someone you feel you can talk to about things?

PUTTING IT ALL TOGETHER

If you decide not to use the services of a designer, or indeed have a design drawn up and then choose to develop the realisation of the design yourself, the time will come when you will need to take the ideas, needs and desires for your Amazing Space from paper and make them happen on the ground. Ideally you'll have two paper documents from which your space will spring – a drawing and an action plan.

CREATING A SKETCH PLAN

Even for the tiniest of spaces there is something that happens when you start to put things down on paper. From the first roughest sketch, ideas start to develop and practicalities emerge that you need to consider. Not everyone has a visual mind and if you need to bring in outside builders or craftsmen it helps them to understand what you are after.

It is very difficult to imagine scale accurately, so start with a rough sketch of your space's floorplan. Include anything location specific – trees, other nearby buildings, as well as an indication of where the sun rises and sets. Sketch out how you imagine the interior structure, but keep it very simple at this point. This initial rough sketch can be on any old paper, but when you start getting specific use squared or graph paper – you don't want to be too worried about things like scale at this stage, the only thing you need to remember is to sharpen your pencil!

After you have made this initial rough sketch, buy yourself a scale ruler. These look slightly scary at first but are actually not at all, and I guarantee that you will become very attached to it. There are different scales that you can use and it is best that they are the relevant size for your project, otherwise you'll end up with a drawing 5cm square. Common scales are 1:5 1:10 or 1:20. By using the correct side of the scale rule you will be easily be able to scale up and down from the measurement on the plan to its reality in meters and centimetres, and mark clearly on your plan what ratio or scale you are using.

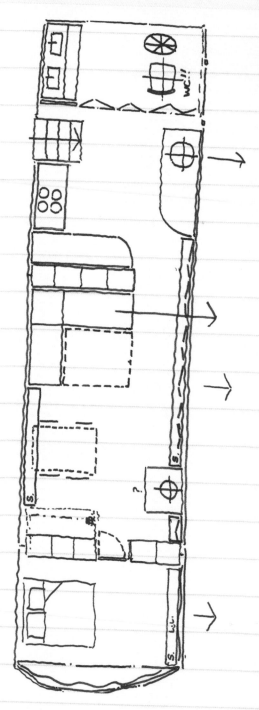

For the Majestic Bus (p150) George drew a rough sketch breaking down the internal layout. Though this would change considerably when the space was assessed in detail, it proved a helpful starting point.

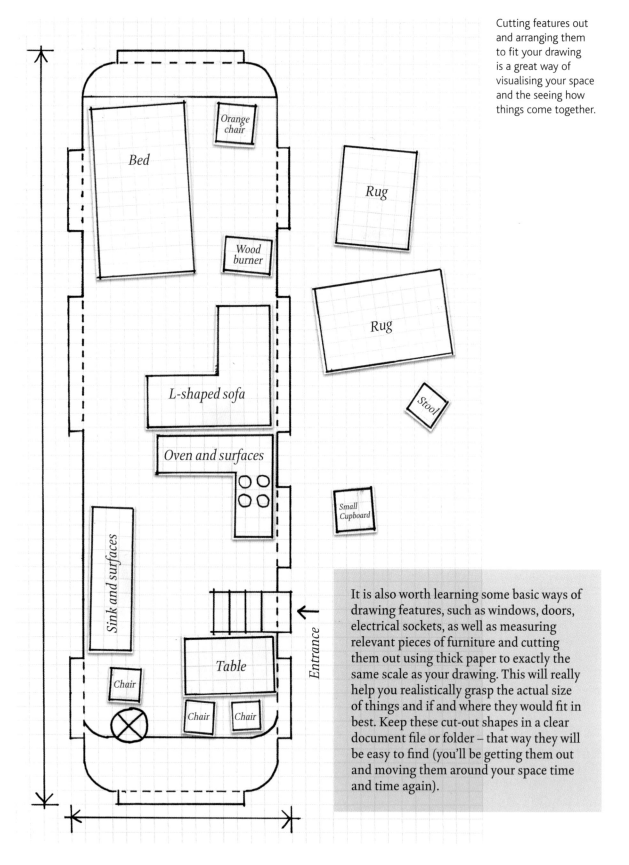

Cutting features out and arranging them to fit your drawing is a great way of visualising your space and the seeing how things come together.

It is also worth learning some basic ways of drawing features, such as windows, doors, electrical sockets, as well as measuring relevant pieces of furniture and cutting them out using thick paper to exactly the same scale as your drawing. This will really help you realistically grasp the actual size of things and if and where they would fit in best. Keep these cut-out shapes in a clear document file or folder – that way they will be easy to find (you'll be getting them out and moving them around your space time and time again).

DRAWING UP AN ACTION PLAN

An action plan is in essence a check list of what needs doing, when. This might sound exceptionally obvious but unless you have really thought through how to do things, and in what order, all sorts of problems can crop up, potentially costing you both time and money. An action plan doesn't need to be a great big, in-depth document – it can be like a holiday luggage list – just a simple A to B plan that helps you to ensure that you are able to get to where you want with your plans with a minimum amount of fuss and costly mistakes.

A SAMPLE ACTION PLAN

Here is a basic guide as to the logical stages that you will need to go through in order to give your project every chance of success. The construction stages here are given for a small outside building such as a shed or garden office – they are not universally applicable to all Amazing Space type builds but nevertheless form a sensible plan of progressing the project. If the project is particularly complex it may require many different tradespeople to work on it and it might be worth considering employing a project manager to help you with the sequencing of works (a job that your architect or designer could fulfil, should you have decided to engage one).

DESIGN STAGES

1. Finalise your concept design and sketch onto a plan. ☐

2. Investigate whether planning permission is needed. If in doubt, take your initial sketches along to your planning office. ☐

3. Start to prepare a preliminary budget – it's no use having a wonderful design if it can't be afforded. Builders will often give you a preliminary estimate of the works, or you may wish to do this yourself (see budgeting overleaf). ☐

4. Work up your detailed technical design from the concept drawing that you are happy with, engaging a designer or architect if needed. Submit these plans for planning application to the relevant authorities if necessary. ☐

BUILDING STAGES

1. Clear the site and excavate groundworks/foundations ☐

2. Lay any drainage ☐

3. Lay the foundations ☐

4. Build the main walls ☐

5. Build the roof structure ☐

6. Apply the roof covering ☐

7. Install windows and doors ☐

8. Affix drainpipes and guttering ☐

9. 1st fix plumbing, heating and electrics ☐

10. Insulate the build ☐

11. Plaster throughout ☐

12. Insert internal woodwork ☐

13. Install kitchens and bathrooms ☐

14. Connect drainage ☐

15. 2nd fix, plumbing, heating and electrics ☐

16. Decorate throughout ☐

⚠

BUILDING REGULATIONS

Remember too that even if you don't need planning permission, aspects of your project may be subject to building regulations. Areas such as fire safety, electrical safety, structure, toxic substances, ventilation, drainage, glazing, heating appliances are all subject to certification and must comply with building regulations.

BUDGETING

Getting the right balance between setting a realistic budget and 'sticking your head in the sand' and just thinking everything will be alright in the end are opposing budget management styles. It is especially hard when you have set your heart on something and want to make it work no matter what. In this case it is very easy to not think sensibly about the true cost of something. For some people that isn't really a worry, but not many of us want our Amazing Space to become a source of financial or any other kind of stress.

Even if your plan involves you doing the work yourself, without any additional labour costs, spending time researching the cost of materials is essential, as is record keeping as to what you actually have spent. All professional and skilled help comes with a cost, as do building regulations and planning permission. You can help yourself keep those costs to a sensible level by researching basic information yourself and submitting your applications in the correct form with the correct amount of detail.

But when it comes to budgeting, indeed when it comes to planning your project from start to finish, I am a great fan of starting a project book to keep all your information in one place. Many of the projects in the book did exactly this – it is a fantastic way to help you think in a logical way, make notes and sketches and to keep a thorough track on spending.

BUDGETING ESSENTIALS

The key questions that you need to ask yourself or consider regarding the budget are: How much can I afford to spend, and is this budget realistic for the work involved? Rather than guess, ask yourself honestly if you know the cost of the materials that you'll need. Get fixed price quotations, set up a simple spreadsheet with your budget and log all your expenditure against this. Try to keep as tight a control on this as possible, particularly at the beginning of the project, where early overspending could mean that you won't be able to afford a key feature or piece of essential construction.

Don't forget that most builders will quote net prices, which means that VAT will need to be added. Connecting utilities to your build is often more costly than you might realise, so do try and get a quotation for this early on. And whatever you do, build a contingency fund into your budget – you may well need it for any of those unexpected extra costs!

FEES

Fees should be agreed before any work commences. If any friends or neighbours have had similar works carried out, it is a good idea to check what sort of level of fees that they paid.

Fees can be:

★ A lump sum charge – a one-off charge for carrying out all of the design works – get a list of what is included.

★ A percentage of the final cost of the building work.

★ Agreed time charges e.g. £100 per hour – try and get some indication of the hours that are expected to be charged. You might also ask for a running total of the hours worked to be submitted with each fee invoice. It is also useful to get some sort of expected limit.

HEALTH *and* SAFETY

It is easy to think that in a small backyard style project this doesn't apply, but even the tiniest of projects requires a practical and sensible approach to health and safety. Remember that, if you are project managing your build, you are responsible for the safety of everybody on your site – it is therefore up to you to see that you plan, manage and monitor it so that it is safe and that any risks have been minimised.

ALWAYS:

Wear a hard hat in any situations where something might fall on your head or injure your head in some way.

Wear appropriate clothing including boots with a toecap.

Wear goggles when using power tools.

Wear gloves when moving materials.

Wear ear protectors when operating or near loud machinery.

Wear a mask when spraying paint, gluing, or sawing wood – fine dust is a danger from all woods not just MDF.

Carry heavy loads responsibly. Ask yourself – is there another way that you could move the item, such as a trolley or a lever?

Keep a properly stocked first aid box and make sure that everyone working on the project knows where it is.

For further information on all of the above along with specific guidelines, check out the Health and Safety executive website www.hse.gov.uk.

INDEX

Page numbers in *italic* refer to the illustrations

PICTURE CREDITS

Excepting the imagery listed below, all photography featured within the pages of this book has been taken by Ben Anders.

1 Matt Melrose, www.leafstorm.com; 4 above centre www.TheRosebery.com; 4 second line left www.studiomyerscough.com; 4 second line centre Photographer Natalie Orchard; 4 second line right Plum Pictures; 4 third line left interiors designed, constructed and fitted AMERICAN RETRO CARAVANS LTD at the ARC WORKSHOP www.arcairstreams.co.uk/ Photography: www.jsphillips.co.uk; 4 third line centre Plum Pictures; 4 third line right Roger Davies/ The Interior Archive; 4 bottom left LAMP Architects/ Photography: www.fionamurray.com; 6 UNP; 8-9 Getty Images; 10 www.arcairstreams.co.uk/ Photography: www.jsphillips.co.uk; 10 right www.platform5architects.com/ alanwilliamsphotography.com; 11 centre Designed by Sam Booth of ECHO, units 1 and 2 Clarebrand Castle Douglas DG7 3AH/ Euan Adamson Photography; 12 right Plum Pictures; 13 centre LAMP Architects/ Photography: www.fionamurray.com; 13 centre Plum Pictures; 13 below Sawday's Canopy & Stars/ www.canopyandstars.co.uk; 14 left copyright Luminair Ltd.; 14 right www.studiomyerscough.com; 15 second down Photographer Natalie Orchard; 15 third down www.christianschallert.com; 16 Matt Melrose, www.leafstorm.com; 17 right Plum Pictures; 17 below Andrew Ogilvy; 18-19 Louise Begbie; 20 centre Lousie Begbie; 21 above right copyright Luminair Ltd.; 21 centre Designed by Sam Booth of ECHO, units 1 and 2 Clarebrand Castle Douglas DG7 3AH/ Euan Adamson Photography; 22 above & 23 below Photo: Peter Lundstrom, WDO – www.treehotel.se; 22 below & 23 above Photo: Fredrik Broman, Human Spectra - www.treehotel.se; 24 – 25 Getty Images; 26 above right Plum Pictures; 26 centre Photographer Natalie Orchard; 26 left and right Getty Images; 27 above left Andrew Ogilvy; 27 above right www.TheRosebery.com; 27 centre right interiors designed, constructed and fitted AMERICAN RETRO CARAVANS LTD at the ARC WORKSHOP www.arcairstreams.co.uk/ Photography: www.jsphillips.co.uk; 28 Photographer Natalie Orchard; 30 above Photographer Natalie Orchard; 30 below Plum Pictures; 31 Photographer Natalie Orchard; 32 Photographer Natalie Orchard; 33 above Paula Red/ Mainstreamimages; 33 below left Simon Upton/The Interior Archive; 33 right Simon Upton/The Interior Archive; 34-38 interiors designed, constructed and fitted AMERICAN RETRO CARAVANS LTD at the ARC WORKSHOP www.arcairstreams.co.uk/ Photography: www.jsphillips.co.uk; 35 Illustration Louise Bagbie; 35 left Plum Pictures; 39 Interior designed by ACME studios but constructed and fitted by AMERICAN RETRO CARAVANS LTD at the ARC WORKSHOP www.arcairstreams.co.uk/ Photography: www.jsphillips.co.uk; 40 www.therosebery.com; 41 Plum Pictures; 42-46 Andrew Ogilvy; 47 left Simon Upton/The Interior Archive; 47 above right Photographer Anouk De kleermaeker/ Taverne Agency. Producer: Yvonne Bakker; 47 below right Photographer Hotze Eisma/ Taverne Agency. Producer; Reineke Groters; 50 Illustration Louise Begbie; 53 Plum Pictures; 55 above right & below left Fritz von der Schulenburg/The Interior Archive; 55 below right www.ipcsyndication.com; 56-57 Getty Images; 58 centre left Photographer Tina Hillier; 58 below left www.christianschallert.com; 58 below right Narratives / Alun Callender; 58 above right YO! Home (prototype), photographed Sep 2012; 59 below right Getty Images; 59 above right Ray Main/ Mainstreamimages/belrepayre.com; 59 above left; YO! Home (prototype), photographed Sep 2012; 60-64 www.christianschallert.com; 65 above Christopher Simon Sykes/The Interior Archive; 65 below left Narratives / Jan Baldwin; 65 below Tom Scott/The Interior Archive; 66-67 Photographer Tina Hillier; 73 all pictures YO! Home (prototype), photographed Sep 2012; 77 Illustration Louise Begbie; 80 above Eric Morin/The Interior Archive; 80 below left Adrien Dirand/Jean-Marc Palisse/Cote Paris/Interior Archive; 80 right Fabienne Delafraye/Maison Magazine/Interior Archive; 85 below left Fabienne Delafraye/Maison Magazine/Interior Archive; 85 below right Nicolas Tosi, Jo Pesendorfer/Cote Paris/ Interior Archive; 85 above Photographer Mikkel Vang/Taverne Agency. Producer: Helen Redmond; 86-87 Getty Images; 88 above left Sawday's Canopy & Stars/ www.canopyandstars.co.uk; 88 above right GAP Interiors/Jumping Rocks Photography; 88 bottom right Plum Pictures; 89 above right Getty Images; 89 below right Marie Pierre Morel / Côté Ouest / Interior Archive; 90 – 94 LAMP Architects/ Photography: www.fionamurray.com; 95 above Photographer Nathalie Krag/Taverne Agency/ Producer Tami Christiansen; 95 below & centre Simon Upton/The Interior Archive; 95 below Interior Archive; 96-98 Photographer Tina Hillier; 99 above Photographer Jansje Klazinga/Taverne Agency/ Producer: Emmy van Dantzig; 99 below left Lisa Keome/Maison Magazine/Interior Archive; 99 right Narratives / Robert Sanderson; 109 below left Vincent Knapp/The Interior Archive; Photographer Prue Ruscou/Taverne Agency/ Producer; Shannon Fricke; 109 above right Photographer Mikkel Vang /Taverne Agency/ Producer: Helen Redmond; 109 below right; 114-115 © James Brittain / VIEW; 116 above left Designed by Sam booth of ECHO, units 1 and 2 Clarebrand Castle Douglas DG7 3AH/ Euan Adamson Photography; 116 centre left www.platform5architects.com/ alanwilliamsphotography.com; 116 below left Dennis Gilbert/ View/ Mainstreamimages; 116 above right Sheepskin Ltd; 116 centre right Plum Pictures; 117 above right Photographer: Jansje Klazinga/ Taverne Agency/ Producer: Emmy van Dantzig; 117 below right GAP Interior Images Ltd; 122 -125 www.studiomyerscough.com; 123 Illustration Louise Begbie; 127 Illustration Louise Begbie; 132 -133 www.platform5architects.com/ alanwilliamsphotography.com; 134 – 138 above © Luminair Ltd.; 137 below Sheepskin Ltd; 139 below left Photography: Anouk de Kleermaeker/ Producer Leoni Mooren; 139 above Photography: Marjon Hoogervorst/ Taverne/ Producer Tatjana Quax; 139 right Photographer: Mikkel Vang / Taverne Agency/ Producer: Helen Redmond; 140 -144 Designed by Sam booth of ECHO, units 1 and 2 Clarebrand Castle Douglas DG7 3AH/ Euan Adamson Photography; 142 above Plum Pictures; 142 below illustration Louise Begbie; 145 above left DURAT kitchen/ Private kitchen in Turku, Finland / Photography by Studio Re/ Interior design by Pirkko-Liisa Topelius; 145 centre Luke White/ The Interior Archive; 145 right Richard Powers; 145 below

Photographer Nathalie Krag/ Taverne Agency/ Producer: Tami Christiansen; 146-147 Getty Images; 148 above left Plum Pictures; 148 centre left Getty Images; 148 below left Getty Images; 148 above right Narratives / Polly Eltes;149 above right Plum Pictures; 149 above left Alderto Norsto; 149 below left Philip Dove; 149 above right Ray Main/ Mainstreamimages/ Designer: steve-edge.com; 149 centre Getty Images; 149 below right Ray Main/Mainstreamimages; 150 Plum Pictures; 151 Illustration Louise Begbie; 151 below Plum Pictures; 152-153 Sawday's Canopy & Stars/ www.canopyandstars.co.uk; 153 below left Plum Pictures; 154 above Photography: Nathalie Krag/ Taverne/ Producer Tami Christiansen; 154 below Thomas Mayer_Archive; 155 above Thomas Mayer_Archive; 155 below Ray Main/ Mainstreamimages/ Baileyshomeandgarden.com; 156-160 Plum Pictures; 159 Illustration Louise Begbie; 160 below left Photographer Tina Hillier; 160 above right & 161 above www.ipcsyndication.com; 161 below Thomas Mayer_Archive; 166-167 Photographer Tina Hillier; 168 Alderto Norsto; 169 Illustration Louise Begbie; 170 above left and below left Plum Pictures; 170 above right Photographer Dana van Leeuwen/ Taverne Agency/ Producer: Jessica Bouvy; 170 below right Photographer Mikkel Vang/Taverne Agency; 171 above Fritz von der Schulenburg/The Interior Archive; 171 below Photographer and Producer: Ngoc Minh Ngo/Taverne Agency; 172 – 175 Sawday's Canopy & Stars/ www.canopyandstars.co.uk; 176-177 Getty Images; 179 Illustration Matt Melrose, www.leafstorm.com; 181 Plum Pictures; 182 Plum Pictures; 183 Illustration Louise Begbie; 184, 186 Illustration Matt Melrose, www.leafstorm.com; 187 Plum Pictures

ACKNOWLEDGEMENTS

We would both like to thank everybody who has played their part in the big job of capturing the essence of Amazing Spaces in book form. To our agents Rosmary Scoular and Ivan Mulcahy, for steering us along and getting things happening. To our publishers Quadrille, for all their hard work in pulling everything together in such a short space of time – to Jane O'Shea for commissioning, Helen Lewis for putting together such a great visual team, Simon Davis for threading the whole thing together, Nicola Ellis for her stunning design and to Ben Anders for his beautiful photography. Thanks also to Ed Griffiths in advance for getting the word out and to Aysun Hughes for all her work on the book's production.

This book wouldn't have been possible if it wasn't for the huge success of the TV series, so a big thank you to Channel 4, to our Commissioning Editor Kate Techman and everyone at Plum Pictures. To Will Daws, Lizzy Wingham, Heather Brown, Angie Cox, Anna Greenaway, Kirsten Taylor, Peter Jones, Scott Corben, Charlotte Numan, Harriette Arthur, Rebecca Magill, and Katy Wingrove – for all the hard work putting the show together and for all their help pulling together the contributors from both series that feature here. A big thanks also to the crew and editors who make the TV series look so beautiful – to Chris Smith, Tim Pitot, Mark Collins, Mac Mackenzie, Roy Williams and everybody at Leafstorm and Halo Post Production. And not forgetting William Hardie and his team for their energy, ideas, fresh thought and great coffee!

For George: First and foremost I'd like to offer a big thanks to my family, for all their support and understanding of this crazy journey. Thanks again to everyone at Plum and Channel 4 for their hard work in getting this off the ground and massive thanks to my exceptional co-author Jane Field-Lewis, for all her incredible work turning this book into a reality.

For Jane: Thanks to Emily Lutyens, Heather Thomas and Sarah Riley for their support. And a big thank you to Robert and Matthew, who do get annoyed with me spending too much time in the office concentrating on all this – the best I can do is to produce a book that you think is good! Thanks to George for everything and to Jay Hunt at Channel 4 for seeing the potential of this idea in the first place – I'm very grateful.

Finally, a huge thanks to all the contributors whose passion, creativity and dedication have made Amazing Spaces what it is. Without you none of this would be possible.

First published in 2013 by
Quadrille Publishing Ltd
Alhambra House
27–31 Charing Cross Road
London WC2H 0LS
www.quadrille.co.uk

10 9 8 7 6 5 4 3 2 1

British Library Cataloguing-in-Publication Data
A catalogue record for this book is available from the
British Library.

ISBN 978 184949 339 0

For Plum Pictures
Executive Producer Will Daws
Series Producer Lizzie Wingham
Series Directors Rebecca Magill, Angie Cox,
Anna Greenaway and Scott Corben
Production Manager Heather Brown
Channel 4 Commissioning Executive Kate Teckman

For Quadrille Publishing
Publishing Director Jane O'Shea
Creative Director Helen Lewis
Project Editor Simon Davis
Assistant Editor Romilly Morgan
Designer Nicola Ellis
Assistant Designers Claire Peters, Gemma Hogan
Photographer Ben Anders
Stylist Jane Field-Lewis
Illustrators Louise Begbie and Matt Melrose
Picture Researcher Claire Hamilton
Production Director Vincent Smith
Production Controller Aysun Hughes

Printed and bound in Germany

Channel 4 is a trademark and is used under licence.